BEFORE I FORGET...

GREAT FIGHTS AND FIGHTERS

1939 - 1959

BEFORE I FORGET...

BY

PETER McINNES

CAESTUS BOOKS

BEFORE I FORGET...

PUBLISHED BY CAESTUS BOOKS

TYPESET IN ENGLAND BY CHRISTINE TITCHEN AND PRINTED BY ANTONY ROWE LTD., BUMPERS FARM, CHIPPENHAM, WILTSHIRE, ENGLAND.

First published 1997

Set in Arial Bold

A catalogue record for this book is available from the British LIbrary

ISBN 0 9525301 2 0

BEFORE I FORGET...
Great Fights and Fighters 1939 - 1959
By
PETER McINNES

CAESTUS BOOKS

DEDICATION

This book is for the men who feature in it; not simply the principals in each chapter, but also for the countless others in the supporting caste whose names appear in a subordinate role and for those numerous warriors not mentioned at all who peddled their wares in the roped arenas, because:

'...them was the days when the trade was a trade,
when they fought hard and trained hard and thrived on it rough
when a man wasn't class 'til he knew ALL the moves...'
(from Peter McInnes' 'BALLAD OF THE FIGHT GLOVES')

Many of the names who feature within these pages are no longer with us. I like to think that, when each climbed through the golden ropes of 'The Big Ring in the Sky' and faced their Maker, they were not found wanting.

ACKNOWLEDGEMENTS

For a second time thanks go to Christine Titchen, our typesetter, not least for putting up with my eccentricities.

Also to our printers, Antony Rowe Ltd., who complete their hatrick of super productions for us with 'BEFORE I FORGET...' Then to Colin Bolger of 'Design Matters' for the great art work on the dust-wrapper.

Working on the basis that 'the last shall be first, and the first shall be last', ta and XXXX to my wife, Jane, for putting up with me at all!!

For, saith the Immortal Bard:

'Scorning all treacherous feud and deadly strife,
The dark stiletto and the lethal knife,
We boast a science sprung from manly pride
Linked with true courage and to health allied;
A noble pastime, void of vain pretence
Is the fine old English art of self-defence.'

CONTENTS

INTRODUCTION

Before I forget, I should tell you that the stories which follow were originally penned some thirty-five years ago, then put into book form and published by a firm which went into liquidation a few weeks later. The books were liquified too, the vast majority being paper-pulped to add--albeit minutely--to the company's meagre assets.

Naturally, in the pages which follow I have had to do some updating along the way, but I have always been anxious that the material herein should be one day available to the world at large. So here it finally is!

There are, however, some important points which need to be made in introduction pertaining to the state of Boxing in the period covered and the sorry state of the game to-day. For instance, a World Championship was just that; the ridiculous alphabet associations had not yet come into being; that began with the WBA in 1962 hotly pursued by the WBC in 1963.

Had the controlling bodies stayed steady with those two, the World Boxing Association and the World Boxing Council, things wouldn't have been so bad but, of course, they did not. Came the IBF (International Boxing Federation) and the WBO

(World Boxing Organisation). Sadly, even that wasn't the mushroom in full fruit. Now we have to tolerate further infiltration from things which call themselves the WBU (World Boxing Union), WBF (World Boxing Federation) and IBO (International Boxing Organisation).

Will it end there? I doubt it. Each of these synthetic bodies has its own set of 'world champions', many of whom are nothing more than good eight-rounders. Unless there is legislation in both this country and America to halt this terminal spread, it will kill the noble art (and, don't forget, we discovered America), stone dead.

Another thing: during the period covered herein there were but eight weight divisions: fly, bantam, feather, light, welter, middle, lightheavy and heavyweight. To-day there are no less than seventeen, the lighter ones being divided by only a matter of three to five pounds. Can you imagine--seven different versions of 'world champion' in each of seventeen weight divisions! To me, this adds up to one hundred and nineteen men being able to call themselves 'world champion' where once there were only eight...

Again, until the beginning of this disintegration of sanity, all contests in Britain were staged under the Rules and authority of the British Boxing Board of Control and these contests, of course, sometimes involved both World and European titles. A British referee was the sole arbiter and his status was never questioned. After all, did we not give Boxing to the rest of the world?

But, for years now, any contest staged in Britain involving some version of a world title has to be fought under the rules of the particular Body involved. Needless to say, these each vary in some degree though all involve a referee who does not score and three judges sitting ringside close to the ring apron on three sides of the square.

Even allowing for the fact that the scoring of a fight has always been, at any rate to some extent, a subjective matter, this has resulted in chaotic and ridiculous scoring. For instance, one recent big fight which went the full twelve rounds was scored by two judges four points in favour of one contestant, while the third rendered his tally five points in favour of the other man!

The men I wrote about in these pages were fighting men; now they're just memories. Many will note that, of the thirty-seven subjects in these twenty-one chapers, only eight are coloured. To-day, one would be hard-put to find a worthwhile fighting subject who is white!

If the demarcation point was World War II plus the coming of the Welfare State in 1948, it was also about that time that the admission of coloured folk to this country began. To my mind, the last two factors have worked to the detriment of fisticuffs, once an art form and the backbone of old England, as a whole.

Where there once were fight cards all over Britain almost every night of the week with young boxers queueing in hope of getting a substitute job to provide money in order to feed their families, nowadays young males prefer to draw unemployment, housing and other benefits rather than work or fight.

The world seemed a far bigger place in the old days, full of fear and mystery. Yet, of all pastimes, it was professional boxing that was the metaphor of life. Champions were revered, followed around by men and small boys alike. To-day, people abhor a bloody nose yet, in those long-gone days, cauliflower ears and flat noses were badges of honour.

'Change and decay all around I see....' The tentacles of the TV monster now reach to all corners of the earth and, I fear, hold the fistic firmament powerless in their grasp.

If only the B.B.B. of C. (1909) had insisted that the flowering alphabet associations BE AFFILIATED TO THEM, rather than themselves seeking affiliation in the reverse direction, things could have been so very different.

What all this preamble amounts to is that there must be world legislation; one overall governing body, a stabilising of Rules and Regulations and the doing away with the freedom of a person or persons to set up their own allegedly controlling body purely for the sanctioning fees readily obtainable through the putting together of bogus world title fights.

The amateur code has its global set-up in A.I.B.A. (Association Internationale de Boxe Amateur), though this is both shambolic and lacking in integrity.

Association Football, better known as soccer, has its own world body in F.I.F.A. (Federation Internationale de Football Association), so does Cricket with the I.C.C. (International Cricket Conference). Something similar could be done to legitimise professional boxing. But, will it ever come to pass? Human nature being what it is, I doubt it!

CHAPTER ONE: ERIC BOON v. ARTHUR DANAHAR, FOR THE LIGHTWEIGHT CHAMPIONSHIP OF GREAT BRITAIN, AT HARRINGAY ARENA, ON 23 FEBRUARY, 1939.

Eric Boon owed his dynamic punching to the blacksmiths's forge where, as a youth in his home village of Chatteris, he used to hammer away at his father's anvil. Being a blacksmith builds up bulky biceps and big shoulders and, providing you have the necessary confidence to catch your opponents as they move towards you, you can punch far harder than any normal man of your weight.

Young Boon had that confidence. He loved fighting right from his schooldays, and soon after starting work for his father he begged him to allow him to box professionally. A natural lightweight in his early days, Eric received two-and-sixpence for his first local engagement. He punched his way to victory so quickly and so consistently that soon he had to look further afield to find worthy opponents.

Soon he was offered a preliminary bout at the Devonshire Club in Hackney, where the East End fans immediately fell for his devastating punching and all-out aggression. He was offered a second outing there the following Sunday.

Because he could not afford the train fare from Chatteris, yet was determined not to forego the fight, Boon cycled the journey of over seventy miles to London. Again he had the

spectators roaring out their applause and, again a happy victor, he peddled the long journey back to the Cambridgeshire village that same night.

Though he had but recently celebrated his sixteenth birthday, the experts began to speak of him as a certain future champion. They could hardly have guessed that he was destined to become the youngest British champion of all time and that, before his nineteenth birthday, he would be the holder of the Lonsdale Lightweight Belt.

Jack Solomons, then matchmaker at the Devonshire Club, took over the reins as manager. Eric demolished opponent after opponent in quick time, and before long he had earned a rating among the title contenders. He still chalked up one-round KO victories with consummate ease and when he won on points over the reigning champion, Jimmy Walsh in an overweight match, he obviously could no longer be denied the chance of a crack at the title.

However, before he got his reward Dave Crowley annexed the crown. Immediately a challenge was issued to the new champion and that astute promoter, the late Sydney Hulls, secured the pairing for Harringay Arena.

Crowley had been boxing in top-class company for years. He knew all the moves and had the ability to exploit them and, as I recall it, the general consensus of opinion was that his

cleverness would more than outweigh Boon's vastly superior punching-power.

And for ten-and-a-half rounds Crowley chastised his young rival as a master might a pupil. But Eric kept moving forward unchastened by the lesson he was receiving, and in the eleventh he got home the one full-blooded blow that was all he needed. Crowley was nailed with a dynamite-laden right-hander in the solar plexus and he never recovered. By the thirteenth his speed had deserted him; another right caught him flush on the chin and he was down and out. Eric Boon, still two weeks short of his nineteenth birthday, was the new Lightweight Champion of Great Britain!

Meanwhile, the National Sporting Club were sponsoring another nine-stone-niner of outstanding promise. His name was Arthur Danahar, and he had shown brilliant form in winning the amateur title in 1937. Hailing from Bethnal Green, he too was undefeated in the paid ring and had run up fourteen victories in the space of a mere nine months. These wins were gained through the near-perfect use of the old-fashioned straight left, which he used to pave the way for marvellously accurate right crosses which, though they did not carry the power behind a Boon blow, usually were enough at least to drop a man.

The patrons of the N.S.C. where the East Londoner was a regular performer, were in direct contrast to those who supported Boon down in Hackney. They were the well-to-do

'Fancy' as opposed to the shrewd 'cockney.' Both factions considered they had the better man under their wing, so it was natural that the clamour should grow for Boon and Danahar to occupy opposite corners in the same ring.

Quite naturally, Sydney Hulls wanted the match for Harringay, the more so as he had given Boon his title chance. Solomons agreed on Eric's behalf, but Danahar stuck by his allegiance to the Sporting Club and gave its members first option on his services. But the Club matchmaker, John Harding, was also unable to clinch the other half of the match.

The public disliked the delay in arranging the bout, and there was a big outcry in the Press when a wealthy unnamed sportsman offered a colossal purse for the men to meet in private at the Grosvenor Hotel. Date was to be 20 November 1938. The connections of both boxers agreed to this proposal; there were to be heavy sidestakes and it really seemed for a while that this finest 'natural' contest in years would be witnessed only by a select few.

Fortunately, for once Press opinion prevailed and the idea was dropped. Finally, Sydney Hulls announced that, by special arangement with the N.S.C., he would stage Boon v. Danahar under championship conditions at Harringay on 23 February 1939 and the bout marked the first occasion of the televising of a boxing contest in England. Needless to say, it was a complete sellout--indeed, the happenings outside the stadium

on the big night had to be seen to be believed. Champion and challenger alike entered the ring amid wild scenes of enthusiasm.

The champion's pronounced muscularity made him look the stronger of the two and Danahar seemed rather drawn, for it was common knowledge that he had had trouble in making the weight. He was the taller man by an inch or so and also had an advantage in reach.

Referee Mr. W. Barrington Dalby, later famous as a BBC inter-round summariser on Sound Radio, seemed to sense the crowd's excitement, and he got the boxers away after the very briefest of final insructions. The very first minute of the opening round clearly indicated the pattern the fight was to take.

Danahar stood bolt upright as in an oldtime boxing print. Boon, bunched forward, his face set in a grim, relentless snarl, kept rushing in to the attack and Arthur would meet him with perfectly-delivered straight lefts, flush in the centre of the face. The challenger used the ring well, too, and he clearly took the opening round.

A swelling suddenly appeared underneath the champion's left eye in the second--an ominous sign--yet he still kept charging in. Though he succeeded in getting through with a few of his heavy swings, Danahar was never ruffled. His boxing was superb.

Round three found Boon desperately seeking to get close enough to unleash his barrage of hooks to the body; but even at close quarters he found that Danahar was fully capable of looking after himself. By the end of the fourth Eric's eye was completely closed and, with his rival still boxing in copybook fashion, it certainly looked as though he was in for a rare hiding.

For seven rounds the challenger gave an exhibition of academic boxing the like of which I never expect to see again. He just could not be faulted. Few champions indeed would have stood up under the kind of thrashing which Boon was forced to take. By the sixth round Eric's eye, in additon to being closed, was horribly swollen. His right eye was also discoloured while blood flowed freely from his mouth and nose.

But never for a moment did the champion halt in his forward march. He was the titleholder. Before the battle was though, this other fellow would be compelled to acknowlege him as such. The crowd knew only too well that Eric needed to land only one of his devastating blows on a vital spot to change the whole course of the fight, but, even so, Boon had no better than an outside chance to those who wager heavily on glove-fights.

Then, in the eighth, Danahar appeared to hesitate when coming out of a clinch. I believe that he heard one of Boon's seconds shout: 'You've got him, now;' and, so much in command did he feel, that he actually paused to grin down at the champion's worried handlers. For a fraction of a second he left

his chin unguarded, and suddenly a terrific right laid him flat on his back. The East-ender got to his feet at 'eight', but he was badly dazed and almost immediately Boon, his 'killer-instinct' now fully aroused, struck him to the boards again for another long count.

This time the Londoner took the count on one knee. When he regained his feet, it could be seen that, whereas the first punch had stupified him, the second had done much to clear his hazy senses. Backing away, he clinched and spoiled until the bell came to his rescue. Nonetheless, I am sure that had the champion struck near the beginning, instead of towards the end of the round, Danahar would have been knocked out in that session.

Danahar made no attempt to ward off Boon's all-out attack at the start of the ninth, but instead ran into clinches repeatedly in an attempt to stall his opponent off until his own strength had returned. By the time the referee warned him for this infringement, he seemed to have recovered his poise and to be boxing as well as ever. When Arthur did finally open up, he hit Boon on the chin with a short right, causing the champion to sit on the bottom rope and to take a short count. Boon was in the act of rising when Danahar, over-elated at his unexpected success, rushed in and struck him on the chin before the referee had ordered 'Box On'.

This incident annoyed Eric, who crowded his man to the ropes under a hail of blows. Again Arthur went down. By now everyone believed that, if he could last the distance, he must win, so great was the tremendous points lead which Danahar had gained in the first eight rounds. In the tenth the Londoner regained his posture somewhat and with it his beautiful boxing, but Boon was not in the least dismayed and he still kept chasing after his man, though most of his blows which landed were negatived in their power by the clever manner in which Danahar rode them. But, just before the end of the eleventh round, Eric finally caught up with his man.

A left hook struck Danahar on the angle of the jaw and, though the gong rang as he was in the act of falling, I believe it would have been better had he been vanquished there and then. From the twelfth round, the Bethnal Green boy took a really terrific hammering; that power-packed blow had knocked all the fight out of him and he was no longer a force to be reckoned with.

Boon was now opposed only by an almost defenceless target upon which he rained a non-stop stream of heavy punches. Left hook after left hook ripped into Danahar's body, but his courage was monumental and it was astounding to see him absorb so much punishment without going to the boards. Then Boon, for a change, threw a right that landed flush on the chin and sent Arthur crashing for 'nine'. He was soon floored

again for a similar count and it was a miracle that he survived until the end of the round.

I remember feeling certain that the gallant Londoner was done and would be unable to answer the bell for the thirteenth, yet he did so and actually survived the round, though he had to take three more long counts.

When he rose the third time Eric walked into him, sighting only with his right eye--the left one looked exactly like a large dollop of blackberry jam--and blazed away unceasingly as Danahar reeled against the ropes in his endeavour to protect hmself. Once again the bell came to his rescue, so there were now only two more rounds to be completed.

But hardly had the challenger left his stool, at the start of the fourteenth round, than a mighty right swing sent him down in a heap. He just beat the count, but stood swaying defenceless and, before Boon could strike another blow, the referee waved the champion to his corner and indicated that the battle had been won.

Eric Boon had retained his title after one of the greatest lightweight clashes of all time. The fighter had beaten the boxer, yet he had been forced to take a heap of punishment in so doing, while his nineteen-year-old challenger had given a display of superlative skill combined with raw courage seldom equalled in prize-ring history.

The best of friends, both Boon and Danahar went on to have plenty more successes and take part in many more fine fights, yet neither of them was ever quite as good again. The magic spark of genius had been banished for ever by the cruel whip of punishment. And I say this despite the fact that Boon went on to win the Lonsdale Gold Belt outright in the near record time of eleven months and twenty-four days by knocking out Dave Crowley for the second time (this time in seven rounds) ten months later.

There was an amusing sequel to the Boon-Danahar fight that same night, when Boon was taken to hospital to have his injured eye attended to. A doctor, eyes shining and cheeks flushed, took Eric into the surgery, glanced at his countenance and murmered: 'That's a nasty looking wound my lad, but it's not half as bad as one I saw a chap get earlier tonight. I've just seen Boon beat Danabar at Harringay and it was a simply terrific fight'.

'Oh really?' said Boon quietly. Something in his tone must have caused the doctor to take a second look, for he suddenly yelled: 'YOU ARE Eric Boon!'

'Well,' grinned Eric, 'if I'm not there's something mighty funny going on around here!'

On the Monday following their great contest, Boon and Danahar met again at the National Sporting Club, when the champion presented Arthur with a silver cigarette casket in token of his admiration for his great performance in defeat. Making a

short speech, he said that if he had had to lose his championship, he could have wished for no finer conqueror than Danahar. The East Londoner, replying, said that he was quite satisfied that he had gone down to a better man on the night.

I feel it would be wrong to end this chapter without recalling that, seven years later, the pair met again in the Harringay ring. But by then, though still good fighters, they were no longer stars and their bout was in support of the Mills-Woodcock pairing. The magic was gone; scarcely anyone got excited when Danahar gained his revenge through a fifth-round knockout. However, there was more to it than that for, up to the time of the knockout, Arthur looked like being beaten decisively.

By the end of the fourth he had been on the canvas several times, and there seemed more than an outside chance that he would not answer the bell for the fifth. This, of course, was in complete contrast to the pattern of their first battle, when Danahar had boxed the ears off Eric in the early rounds. But both were by now fully fledged welterweights.

Anyway, we should have known the Londoner better than to think, even for a minute, that he would admit defeat before the referee had named his opponent winner. He left his stool for the fifth round slowly--I now realise that he must have been setting himself to throw one final, desperate punch. Boon, sensing the kill, hurtled towards him and Arthur put his all into a huge blow

to the mid-section. It dropped Boon like a sack and he was counted out, writhing on the canvas.

Boon rang down the curtain on his fighting life when, in April 1948, he put up another pulsating performance. At Harringay he faced a stocky Frenchman, Robert Villemain, who reigned as European and French welter-weight champion. After giving promise of scoring a great win, Boon was knocked out with only five seconds remaining of the tenth and final round. This was certainly one of the finest non-title fights I have ever been privileged to watch.

Be that as it may, memories fade and time marches on. Yet I know that whenever I read of or hear the names Boon or Danahar mentioned in the future, I shall think of that glorious night way back in 1939 when Eric triumphed in the fourteenth round.

CHAPTER TWO: 1940--THE FABULOUS HENRY ARMSTRONG--CHAMPION AT THREE WEIGHTS, PLUS AN ABORTIVE ATTEMPT AT A FOURTH WORLD CHAMPIONSHIP.

Quite the most amazing record ever amassed by a pugilist is held by the Negro, Henry Armstrong. At one and the same time 'Homicide Hank' held three world titles--an unequalled feat. The only other man ever to reign supreme at three different weights was the immortal Cornishman, Bob Fitzsimmons, who besides once being titleholder at middle and lightheavyweight, was also the only British-born boxer to capture the heavyweight championship of the world. But Fitz held his titles separately.

Sugar Ray Robinson almost succeeded in emulating Armstrong and Fitzsimmons in that respect, for, already having been the champ among the welters and middleweights, he attempted to wrest the lightheavyweight crown from Joey Maxim during the summer of 1952, only to be overcome by the heat in round thirteen when he looked a certain winner.

Although, for Armstrong, 1939 was perhaps a more successful year than 1940, I have decided to devote the basis of this chapter to the latter year for one outstanding reason--it was in that year that the 'Human Buzzsaw' took a crack at a fourth world title, the middleweight, and only failed to win it on account of the rendering of an extraordinary drawn verdict.

Born Henry Jackson in the deep south of Mississippi, Armstrong's father was a share-cropper in the cotton fields, but, with a growing family to support, he went north to St.Louis in Missouri. There Henry fought his way through the local talent until he had run out of opponents. He met a professional fighter named Harry Armstrong, and they decided to make their way to California where there were far better opportunities.

In San Francisco, a hot-bed of boxing from bareknuckle days, Henry continued as an amateur, only because he was still too young to obtain a licence to box professionally. Together they found a manager of sorts called Tom Cox, who had a mania for economy. Cox was aghast when he first offered Henry a meal, for he thought the coloured boy would never stop eating. Yet he needed all the energising foods he could get to replace the force and fury he expended in the ring.

To put a curb on this expensive habit, Cox entered Henry in a competition to decide the composition of the American team for the Olympic Games. He put him in the bantams, in spite of the fact that the boy was a natural featherweight. So Henry had to starve himself, to by-pass meals by chewing gum and by cutting drinking to a minimum. It was high degree torture that only increased each time he was due to box.

No wonder that he failed to make the Olympic side, and no wonder that he was knocked out in his first professional contest in 1932. 'We'll change your name', declared Harry

Armstrong. 'You've been knocked cold as Jackson, let's see what you can do with mine.' And that is how Henry Armstrong came into being.

There was a well-known manager named Eddie Mead, who made it known that he was most impressed with Armstrong's potential. Eventually, with the aid of singer Al Jolson, he bought Cox out. From then on Armstrong's fortunes took a turn for the better. Perhaps the devastating effect of his punching, together with his bobbing and weaving style, prevented him from receiving the full brunt of the blows fired back at him by his rivals in sheer desperation.

Soon his nicknames were on everyone's lips, for he hounded opponents along the ropes, caught them, hammered them and brought them down or else drove them into a corner to beat them into a state of helplessness. He was too good for the fighters and boxers alike.

When Armstrong met Baby Arizmendi he was introduced to a new style of fighting. Up to then he had used his speed and hurricane, non-stop hitting to put rivals out of their stride, followed by his punching-power to finish them off. The Mexican marched straight into Henry and started punching it out with both hands. There was nothing to do but follow suite.

Arizmendi won their first meeting by a shade, and he also got a doubtful verdict in a return. But in their third set-to Armstrong was an easy winner, which proved that he was

learning fast. After he had outpointed Mike Belloise, Mike Jacobs matched Henry against world featherweight champion Petey Sarron in a title bout on 29 October 1937.

Sarron, a tough, hard little warrior, fought desperately to keep his crown, but he could not stand up to the blistering, unceasing fire of Armstrong. Henry pumped an endless stream of blows into his game rival and, in the sixth round, Petey was battered to his knees and counted out.

Though world champion at last, it was at what was, by now, a killing weight and Henry had had to starve and thirst to make it. Now perhaps he could have a rest, for he had been fighting at the rate of once every fortnight for the past year or more. The frequent bouts and the very fury of his fighting had helped with the weight-making, but it had been a tremendous strain.

How happy he must have felt when manager Mead told him that his next fights would be as a lightweight, for this gave him an added margin of nine pounds. But he still got no rest from the ring. Three weeks after beating Sarron he was back in action and, during the next seven months, won fourteen bouts, all but one inside the distance. Then he had his second championship match.

Yet not for the lightweight title! Promoter Mike Jacobs knew that the champion, Lou Ambers, was still capable of outboxing Armstrong, whereas Barney Ross, the welterweight

king, was starting to slide. They hired the big open-air Bowl on Long Island for that one. For the first time in history, a featherweight champion was taking on the welterweight title-holder.

Henry swarmed over him from start to finish. Smart boxer that he was--and Barney had been lightweight kingpin before annexing the welterweight title--the heavier man had to wage an uphill battle all the way. Ross refused to surrender; he stood up for the full fifteen rounds under the most outrageous battering any champion has ever had to endure. He collapsed at the final bell and never fought again.

That was on the last day of May 1938. On l7 August the same year Armstrong outpointed Ambers to win the lightweight title, which feat made him appear superhuman! Within two months he had relinquished his featherweight laurels--having no further need to undergo the purgatory of making nine-stone--and, by the end of the year, he had already successfully put his welterweight crown on the line twice. It is significant that the second of these defences was against Ceferino Garcia, whom Armstrong walloped without much trouble on this occasion.

And so to 1939, during which year Armstrong made no less than eleven victorious defences of his welterweight title, winning all but three of them inside the distance. True, in August, he dropped the lightweight crown in a return with Ambers, but neither he nor manager Mead was much perturbed

by this. For by now, Homicide Hank preferred to do his battling in the welterweight class where he had plenty of latitude to satisfy the enormous appetite and even greater thirst which he had developed in the days of those nightmarish battles with the scales.

Every fight was a title bout then and, in May 1939, Henry came to England to meet our own welterweight champion, Ernie Roderick, for promoter Johnny Best at Harringay Arena. Nobody who, like myself, saw Armstrong's astonishing performance that night will ever forget his amazing exhibition of perpetual motion.

While the challenger was making his way to the ringside, the champion was indulging in a fast spell of shadow-boxing in his dressing room. As he came down the aisle towards his corner, Henry was jigging on his toes and punching the air fast with either hand, and he kept this up after he had climbed through the ropes. Except for the few moments he stood still to allow his gloves to be tied, Armstrong was perpetually on the move, a most extraordinary thing when one naturally expects a man to conserve every ounce of his energy at such a time, in readiness for the trial ahead.

But Hank was no ordinary person. Built superbly for the style of fighting which he adopted, he had an exceedingly large heart, which it was necessary to work up to a fast beat before its owner could use his limbs at the terrific pace he demanded of them, and also get full power behind each of his speedy

punches. All this preliminary exercise was essential so that Henry could leave his corner at the opening gong and move straight into action at top speed. Even so, he usually finished a fight at an even faster pace than that at which he began.

Roderick was a good British champion and that night he fought well; probably as well as any opponent in the world could have done, yet he could never match the will-o'-the-wisp pace and inexhaustible energy of the mighty American.

After the fight was over, Roderick confirmed to me that his tactics had been to wait for this human hurricane to blow itself out and, by the time he realised that this was a forlorn hope, it was too late to do anything about it. For the last rounds he kept himself going, I swear, only by dousing his head into an ice-bucket between rounds.

Right eye closed, left eye cut, eyebrows and cheeks badly swollen, our outclassed champion looked like the victim of a thousand wasp stings. The referee's verdict came as a mere formality, with Ernie staggering across the ring to shake hands with his composed conqueror even before the referee had given his decision.

Yet Roderick had never once been on the canvas; the real merit of that performance can only be judged when viewed against the background of Armstrong's fantastic record. For two years before that bout he had been undefeated, and had crammed in forty-four contests, clubbing his way to knockouts in

in thirty-nine of them! In addition, against Roderick, he had been the lighter man by a matter of ten-and-three-quarter pounds.

Henry Armstrong, the 'Human Dynamo', didn't pick easy opponents. He treated them all alike, the fighters, the punchers, the boxers, the 'fancy-dans', 'cuties' and the 'runners'. If any further proof of this was needed, combined with his willingness to put the ten-stone-seven title at stake against all-comers, then that proof was forthcoming in 1940. But the end of the year saw him lose the coveted crown--chiefly because the supply of that unknown fuel which makes for nervous energy was rapidly running out.

The New Year saw the Armstrong entourage in St. Louis to meet one Joe Ghnouly on 4 January. Joe was reckoned not much of a technician, but he was a terrific puncher with the right hand. It was thought that Henry's ever-moving-forward style might lead him into taking a blow which, if it landed propertly, would certainly spell 'curtains' for the champion.

Ghnouly, however, was completely overwhelmed by Armstrong's speed and, on the few occasions when he did manage to wind-up his famed right, it landed on thin air or on the back of Hank's shoulders. He was counted out in the fifth round--not from any one particular blow, but rather as a victim of sustained punishment, coupled with extreme exhaustion. Three weeks later Armstrong went in against Pedro Montanez in New York for Mike Jacobs. Now this Montanez had class: he could

punch and he could box and he was rated leading contender tor the title at that time. Pedro was in the hunt for a few rounds, but then, like all the others, he found himself unable to contend with the champion,'s pace. Finally, being unable to slow his rival down in the least, Montanez was knocked out in the ninth.

In that year, there were two claimants to the Middleweight Championship of the World. They were Ceferino Garcia who, you will remember, had been outpointed by Armstrong in a welter title clash towards the end of 1938, and Al Hostak: Garcia's claim was much stronger for he had come to power by defeating Fred Apostoli, who had taken the title away from France's Marcel Thil, back in 1937.

Contracts were signed for Garcia to defend his crown against the welterweight champion in Los Angeles on I March, and Henry was made a hot favourite on account of his previous comfortable victory over Ceferino. The bout was a terrific attraction, for never before in the history of the game had any scrapper fought for a world title at four different weights.

Armstrong conceded nearly a stone in weight, for he came in at inside the welterweight poundage, yet he swarmed over Garcia in each of the rounds and seemed to have won by an even larger margin than on the occasion of their first meeting. The verdict of a draw (which meant that Garcia was still champion) met with howls of protest, Press critics being almost

unanimous in their view that Armstrong should have been named the winner.

He never got another crack at the eleven-stone-six title, for, during the next few months, he was far too busy defending his own crown. Then, with the falling of autumn leaves, the writing was on the wall for all to see and suddenly he was no longer a champion at all. But first....

Paul Junior tried his luck in Boston. A strong, tough, two-fisted fighter in the Armstrong mould, Junior ran out of steam in the seventh round after trying to match Henry at his own game. He should've known better!

Next on the list, also in Boston and less than a month later, was Ralph Zanelli. This character was the exact opposite of Junior. A non-puncher, he was extremely crafty and particularly adept at smothering and tying opponents up at close quarters. These tactics were miles off the beam against an adversary of Armstrong's class, and Zanelli bit the dust in the fifth round.

Portland, in June, saw Paul Junior try again. This time he adopted different tactics. Instead of coming out slugging he opened cautiously, presumably in the expectation that the world champion would, sooner or later, leave himself open and allow Paul a real chance of nailing him with a two-handed combination. What happened, though, was that Junior was laid out cold in the third before any such thing happened.

The following month Henry met Lew Jenkins in Madison Square Garden. Jenkins was the reigning lightweight kingpin--and he had all the attributes that go to make a real champion. The old adage that 'a good big'un will always--though I prefer to say nearly always--beat an good little 'un gained weight when Jenkins was licked inside the six rounds. Nonetheless, it was noticeable in this bout that Armstrong, who was the heavier man by several pounds, had to survive some awkward moments.

Phil Furr was battered down in four rounds in Washington, and then it was proved that the pitcher can go to the well too often. For the twenty-first defence of his welter laurels Henry came up against Fritzie Zivic, youngest of three fighting brothers and fully equipped with every trick of the ring.

The brawl took place on 4 October in New York, and it showed everyone but Armstrong that his inner dynamo had begun to lose its speed and power. He lost a grim fifteen rounder, being on the canvas at the final bell, the first time he had been dropped since he was knocked out at the start of his paid career. That was all for 1940, and it was the end of Armstrong the champion.

There was a return three months later, and the fans could scarcely believe their eyes as they watched Henry's pathetic attempts to recapture the title. In the twelfth round Armstrong sank to his knees and the referee waved Zivic to his corner, refusing to let gallant Hank take any more punishment.

Of course, there was the inevitable comeback, but though Armstrong kept on fighting with varying success for another four years, he never got within reach of a title fight again. Finally he was licked by an unknown named Chester Slider in Oakland and, realising at last that he was through, he hung up his gloves for good.

From the milion dollars and more he had earned with his busy fists, only a Cadillac and a few bonds remained. These, like the hordes of friends who had surrounded him in his heyday, soon disappeared.

Yet 'Homicide Hank' still campaigned, but against the devil. He became the Reverend Henry Armstrong, in charge of a Baptist Church in California, and was the leading spirit in the Henry Armstrong Youth Foundation for many years.

CHAPTER THREE: JOE LOUIS v. BILLY CONN: FOR THE HEAVYWEIGHT CHAMPIONSHIP OF THE WORLD AT THE POLO GROUNDS IN NEW YORK, ON 18 JUNE, 1941.

One of the most memorable of all Joe Louis' fights was his first title defence against Billy Conn. Memorable for a number of reasons. First Louis came desperately close to losing his crown, then more than fifty thousand customers witnessed one of the greatest of all heavyweight title fights and finally, the old ring adage that 'a good big 'un will always beat a good little 'un' was once again borne out. On the night of the 18 June 1941, Pittsburgh-born Conn gave the great 'Brown Bomber' a boxing lesson in New York's Polo Grounds, but, in the thirteenth round, he forgot to duck....but I'm leaping ahead.

Round about his nineteenth birthday, Joseph Louis Barrow asked his mother if she would object to his becoming a boxer. 'If that's really what you want to do, go ahead, but remember you must be a good one', she said.

So Joe Louis--to which he trimmed his name for combat purposes--became a boxer and a good one. So good that he was to reign for nearly twelve years on the most coveted throne in sport, during which time he met and defeated every challenger worthy of the description. In all he defended his laurels twenty-five times and broke every record in boxing during his reign,

including the number of his title defences and the amount of money which his fists earned for him.

He met the cream of the heavyweight talent once he moved into big-time boxing in 1935 and, when he retired in 1948, he had been beaten only once in sixty-one professional contests. It was sheer tragedy that he attempted a comeback a year later, for Louis compared favourably with any of his predecessors--those fistic greats about whom old-timers talk with bated breath, such as John L. Sullivan, Jim Corbett, Bob Fitzsimmons, James J. Jeffries, Jack Johnson, Jack Dempsey and Gene Tunney.

During his years of ring activity Joe proved that he possessed all the fighting qualities of a great champion, plus the virtues of a gentleman. He had the punch to give him drawing-power and he had colour because of the sincerity which went into all his ring-work. Also he had the spur of popularity to make him rise to the heights.

Joe was fortunate in the fact that, from the start, he teamed up with Jack Blackburn, a former fighter who had met the best in the lightweight division. They became firm friends and Blackburn found that Louis was ever ready to learn and would never fail to put into practice any advice he was given.

Each time Joe made a mistake, the fault was analysed by the boxer and his trainer and rectified. It was thus never repeated. Very soon after turning professional Louis' quick knockout victories earned him the ring soubriquet of the 'Brown

Bomber'. When Joe fought ex-champion Primo Carnera before he himself won the title, he jabbed at the Italian giant's midsection until he lowered his guard to protect his body. Then Louis unleashed his heavy artillery and the big man suffered a terrrible beating until the referee halted the slaughter.

Max Baer, one of the hardest right-hand punchers in the game, thought that he could lay the young but rapidly rising coloured fighter low. But Joe stood with him and slugged, giving back blow for blow until Baer lost heart. It was all over in four rounds.

Early in Joe's career, when he was still very green, they matched him with the experienced German, Max Schmeling, himself a former world kingpin. The German beat Louis to the punch with a right in the fourth round and Joe went down with a thud. Yet he climbed off the canvas again and again and went on taking a beating for eight more rounds until finally being counted out in the twelfth.

As bad as it was, that beating by Schmeling did not break the 'Brown Bomber's' heart and he was back in the ring only two months later, after which it was success all the way. Yes, Joe Louis could punch all right--his record is proof enough of that. But he did not bludgeon, as did old John L. Sullivan and Jeffries, rather his precision punching was almost too quick for the eye to see and too devastating for the nervous system to absorb.

Louis became feared. Men eager enough to draw the big money for opposing him, were drained of their resistance in the dressing-room before even entering the ring. Others fought in desperation, a fatal thing to do against a cold, calculating fighting-machine like the 'Brown Bomber'.

Not that Joe became world champion the easy way. When he fought Braddock for the title, that wily old campaigner dropped his challenger in the opening round. it was an experience likely to knock the ambition out of any twenty-three-year-old youngster, yet Louis came back and, in the eighth, he had the satisfaction of seeing Braddock lying at his feet--by now just another 'ex-champion!' That was in June 1937 and, between that time and when he put the title on the line against Conn--four years almost to the day, afterwards--he succcessfully defended the treasured championship seventeen times, winning all but two of these engagements inside the distance. He had all but fought himself out of opponents.

Billy Conn's parents had emigrated to America from Ireland shortly after they married. From the age of fiteeen Billy had set his heart on becoming a professional boxer, and it is interesting to note that he is one of the few American boxers who never had an amateur career before appearing in a paid ring.

He was unquestionably the best-looking boxer I ever met, and, according to those most closely associated with him, he was also one of the wildest. At times he could not resist the hot

surge of his Irish blood and, as we shall see, it was this fault that made him literally throw away the world's richest sporting prize--the Heavyweight Championship.

Billy showed absolutely no interest in any other sport except boxing. From the time he first pulled on the gloves he was a dedicated young man, working out in a gymnasium run by Johnny Ray, a friend of his father's and the man who was to become his manager. When he was not in the gym, he was raising hell elsewhere in Pittsburgh and, so wild was he, that the nuns of the Sacred Heart Parochial School asked his parents to take him away. Thus Billy began his career as a professional boxer almost overnight.

It is impossible to list the early bouts in Conn's barnstorming tour of the United States, but he gained vast experience by taking every possible fight--no matter where the venue or how meagre the monetary rewards offered. By 1937 his natural boxing skill was as near perfection as any human being is likely to get such an art. His one failing was that he lacked a KO punch, but, even so, that year he fought the best men in the game and beat them. The National Press began to liken Conn's style to that of ancient James J. Corbett.

The following year Billy won seven fights, then came his big chance against former world middleweight champion, Fred Apostoli, in Madison Square Garden. The youngster caused a sensation, and even seasoned ringsiders were moved to

admiration by his handsome appearance as he entered the ring clad in an emerald-green dressing-gown, with a golden harp embroidered on the back. He waved and grinned, displaying a perfect set of teeth, aquiline features and black, curly hair.

And his boxing lived up to his appearance, for he literally cut Apostoli to ribbons and showed bewildering speed and astonishing boxing ability. The crowd and critics raved about Conn and, a month later, he again gave Apostoli a boxing lesson in a fiteeen-rounder. Mike Jacobs, impresario at the Garden and one of the shrewdest promoters in the history of the fight game, realised that Billy was going to prove almost as big a drawing-card as Joe Louis himself. He therefore matched his find against 'southpaw' Melio Bettina, the world lightheavyweight champion, with the title at stake in Madison Square Garden on 13 July 1939.

The hapless Bettina was scientifically annihilated over fifteen rounds and now, as lightheavy champion, Conn was the toast of the town. He made two successful title defences against Gus Lesnevich--for he had no difficulty whatsoever in coming in a twelve stone seven, the lightheavyweight limit--and then....

Mike Jacobs usually looked on boxers as being little better than perfoming animals who earned him money at the turnstiles. But Conn was an exception and, whenever he fought, Jacobs was to be seen at the ringside cheering wildly. Billy, though hot-tempered, was a lad of great natural charm, and he spent most of his time at Jacobs' country resort, when he was in

New York, and it became common gossip in the fight-game that the promoter intended matching the Irish boy with Louis.

As a build-up to the fight Conn was matched against heavyweights like Bob Pastor, Al McCoy, Lee Savold and Gunner Barlund. He accomplished something Louis had been unable to do by knocking out Pastor, who a few months earlier had taken the champion the full distance; and it became obvious that, when Louis and Conn were brought together, one of the results would be a million-dollar gate.

As soon as the match was clinched, Billy began to shout from the rooftops about how he intended to relieve Louis of his crown. So sure was he of victory, that he went so far as to tell reporters that he would knock the champion out in the twelfth round. Conn trained at Atlantic City, while Joe put in his final preparation at Pompton Lakes.

Then, one evening, the Pittsburgh-Irishman put through a personal call to the champion at his training quarters, and proceeded to tell Louis that, in his opinion, he was a bum and that he intended to tear his head off when they got into the ring.

So confident was Billy Conn on the day of the fight that, instead of resting in his hotel room after the weigh-in, as any normal fighter would do, he went skylarking around the place with brother Jackie. Apparently Billy had disturbed his sleeping brother by squirting some soda-water into his mouth and, when junior recovered, he was wild with rage and chased Billy round

the hotel with a baseball bat--much to the consternation of the fighter's handlers.

Sure enough, the fight drew well over a million dollars and the customers had their moneysworth in thrills. Against custom, the champion entered the ring first with a towel over his head. Blackburn tried to take it from him, but Joe moved away from his trainer to acknowledge the applause. Then Conn came tripping down the aisle.

He, too, received a hero's welcome and he smiled and winked to ringside Press men when he was introduced as 'a most worthy contender'. In the first round Conn was fast--much too fast for Joe to nail him. Billy was in and out, circling first this way, then that, and easily outboxing the much bigger Louis, who outweighed him by almost two stone.

He just didn't give Louis time to get set, though the champion kept stalking forward, throwing out left jabs, but never getting within range to throw a really powerful blow. Conn was on the retreat all the time, yet it was he who did most of the scoring.

Things livened up a lot in the second, when Joe got Billy into his sights for the first time, and caught him with some powerful shots which caused him to run to holds. But Joe wrestled himself free, and at the bell he was freely punishing his rival who looked to be in real trouble at this stage.

Billy made a splendid recovery at the start of the third and, throughout that round and the next, his fast hitting and equally speedy footwork seemed to have Louis bewildered. He broke up each and every one of the 'Brown Bomber's' attacks with consummate ease, all the time expertly hooking and jabbing.

The next three rounds were even, but from the start of the eighth, Conn began to box as only he knew how. Slowly but surely his incredible skill and burning speed took him way into the lead on points. However, he was warned by his seconds at the end of every round not to relax for a moment, for Louis was not only one of the heaviest punchers the fight-game had ever known, he was also one of the finest opportunists. He could spot an opening in the twinkling of an eye and could whip over a punch which, if it landed, would spell curtains for any man in the world.

So much did Conn get on top that, by the eleventh round, he was so 'cocky' and sure of himself that he expressed his intention of knocking Joltin' Joe out. His seconds pleaded with him to be careful--they told him that he was so far ahead on points that he only needed to coast through the remaining rounds to win the decison and the title.

Alas, in the twelfth round Billy landed a left hook which definitely shook the champion and the Irish boy came back to his corner, aglow with elation and excitement. At the beginning of

the thirteenth, Conn was out of his corner before Louis had time to rise from his stool and he cursed Joe loudly for his slowness. The 'Bomber' was never more dangerous than when roused. By this time, Conn's attitude had really angered him.

Conn started to drive hard at Louis again, and he got home with both hands while Joe was concentrating on trying to manoeuvre his rival into a corner. With Billy dancing in and out on his toes, there still seemed to be only one man in it but suddenly, Conn's back hit the ropes, Louis letting rip with a blasting combination of left and rights.

A right uppercut jerked the challenger's head back like a doll at the end of a string before he could contrive a sidestep. And Louis kept after him, throwing punches all the time. Finally, a left hook like a sepia shadow sent Conn on his way to the canvas. Before he hit the deck a following right caught him high up on the cheekbone and that was that--it was all over.

They dragged Conn back to his corner and brought him round. Then he had to taste the cup of real bitterness when he was made to realise that his conceit and folly had deprived him of what could have been his finest hour.

The following year Conn, like the champion, was drafted into the Army: the proposed return contest, which Mike Jacobs had been anxious to stage, had to be postponed indefinitely. I met both Louis and Conn when they were in this country as Servicemen during the war.... Joe, in fact, saw quite a lot of

Bournemouth, my home town. I remember how, one day, we walked together along the two-mile promenade, with all and sundry goggling wide eyed at the famous fighter and/or stopping him to ask for his autograph.

I got a typical Louis answer when I remarked that, day in and day out, this must be very trying on your temper. Slowly Joe drawled: 'Ah guess it's OK by me as long as the people want to know me. It's when they stop caring that ah'll have to start worrying!'

I met Conn one night at Belle Vue, Manchester. If my memory serves me right, it was on 15 September 1944, when Jack London outscored Freddie Mills to win the vacant British and Empire heavyweight titles.

I plucked up sufficient courage to ask Billy what it felt like to be nailed by Louis. He told me that, in his case at any rate, it was a strange feeling. For although, he said, all was blackness as he went down, yet he knew he was on his way to the canvas and was somehow conscious of the tragedy which had overtaken him.

Billy lived high, wide and handsome during the war years. He struck me as being a lot of fun. I liked him immensely, even if he did once remark that my good friend Freddie Mills could never lay a glove on him in fifteen rounds!

When the war was over, Conn and Louis met again in June 1946. By this time the flame of Billy the Kid's brilliance had

burnt itself out and Louis was also past his best. Still, if Joe was poor, Billy was rank shocking. He was knocked out in the eighth round of a dull bout.

Later Conn struck oil in Texas and became a very wealthy man. Louis, crippled by tax debts and confined to a wheelchair, died in Las Vegas in 1981.

CHAPTER FOUR: LEN HARVEY v. FREDDIE MILLS: FOR THE LIGHTHEAVYWEIGHT CHAMPIONSHIPS OF GREAT BRITAIN AND THE BRITISH EMPIRE; ON THE TOTTENHAM HOTSPUR FOOTBALL GROUND ON 20 JUNE, 1942. (THIS BOUT WAS RECOGNISED IN BRITAIN AS BEING ALSO FOR THE WORLD TITLE).

Most fighters carry the mark of their profession on their faces, such as a battered or broadened nose, some white scar-tissue around the eyes or a thickened ear. But not Len Harvey, who fought professionally for well over twenty years and engaged in more than a score of title fights. Watching him, as he served his customers at the Derby Arms in East Sheen, one would never have guessed that, during his long ring career, he engaged in some four hundred battles and won eight titles spread over three different weight divisions.

You would not have dreamt, either, that his first professional fight was at the age of twelve, that he was a champion at twenty-one and that he fought the toughest and best men in the world. But when you know that he was only knocked out once in all those encounters, only twice stopped inside the distance, outpointed on no more than a dozen occasions, it becomes easier to understand why the casual oberver rarely connected him with the hazards and rigours of the ring.

Harvey boxed a draw with Harry Mason for the welterweight title when Freddie Mills was but a six yearold schoolboy--that was in April 1926. In this chapter, I shall tell how the old master undertook that one fight too many after a three year layoff, and so met with his one and only knockout reverse. It is, perhaps, unfortunate that the fistic period covered in my book does not allow me to base this chapter on a Harvey triumph, but Len was far too great a figure to omit, and I believe that he would have appreciated my intention, for he knew well that I was present only as the final curtain fell on his fighting career.

There will always be a champion, and always a challenger to his supremacy. Even while two top men contest the immediate issue, somewhere, maybe a blob among the faces of the vast crowd, or maybe away in some remote village, there is a virile lad who will one day step up to take his turn against the winner. That is the code of the fight-game, that is the way it was with Harvey and Mills. When Len won his first title, in 1929, Freddie watched the boxing from the glass dome on top of the old Bournemouth Winter Gardens. Having no money, he used to make the dangerous climb in order to peer in free!

I think it will be as well if, at this stage, I clear up the muddle concerning British recognition of the Harvey-Mills battle as being for the world championship. Len met the American Negro champion, John Henry Lewis, for his crown at Wembley in 1936, and was beaten narrowly on points. Some three years later

Lewis returned to Britain for a return title contest with Harvey, only to have the British Boxing Board of Control veto the match, when its doctor found fault with the state of the world champion's eyesight. In fact, the coloured man's vision became so impaired that it led to his retirement from the ring as undefeated world's champion. Our Board then decided that the Harvey-McAvoy match in July 1939, already involving two titles, should include the world crown, with the winner having to defend same against an American to be named by the United States authorities. But, instead, the Yanks paired Billy Conn with Melio Bettina in a title bout, and both Harvey-McAvoy and later Harvey-Mills became just a 'British version' of the world championship.

As a boy, Leonard Austin Harvey was retiring and of frail physique, although he was healthy enough. The first time his father took him to the Cosmo Club in Plymouth to watch a boxing show, he recalled feeling sick at the mere sight of two men slugging it out.

Surely, there was more to boxing than that, he thought. Wasn't it known as 'The Noble Art'? So he began to spar with the best at the Club, concentrating on defence, mainly because he was not strong enough to stand up to heavy punches. At the same time he practised body-building so that he would be able to withstand chance blows without any damaging effect. He

perfected a style that enabled him to take only the minimum of punishment.

Len began boxing in the flyweight (or eight stone and under) class. Florence came into his life very early on. The pair were childhood sweethearts and Harvey told a good story of one of his early fights against a tough foreigner at the old Blackrfriars Ring. In those days he was managed by the late Dan Sullivan who, on this occasion, watched the proceedings from the back of the hall.

Sullivan noticed that whenever the boxers went into a clinch, Harvey would look up to the balcony: once he actually winked. Suspiciously following the young boxer's glance, Dan spotted a pretty blonde. Afterwards he gave Len a lecture for jeopardising his own chances, and Florence similar medicine for being there at all. He warned her that this sort of thing could only result in Len's ruin as a boxer, only to get the Florence retort of: 'Then the sooner we get married, the better'.

The manager allowed the happy couple one day's honeymoon--and he sent Len's trainer away with them. Two days after returning home, Harvey gained one of the best of his early wins by vanquishing a dangerous French-man named Kid Nitram.

By the spring of 1929 Harvey had fought his way through all the five lower weight divisions and was campaigning in the middleweight class, where he had established himself as the

outstanding contender for the national title which was then held by Alex Ireland. The champion also held the Empire and European championships, but he was deprived of the lot when Harvey knocked him out in seven rounds in mid-May. And, before the end of the year, Len twice successfully defended his newly-won laurels against Jack Hood, though he forfeited the European crown without a fight, because he could not fit in a defence against a Continental rival.

From this point on the record of Harvey's numerous championship bouts at different weights becomes involved. Suffice it to say that, between the start of 1930 and April '33, when Jock McAvoy wrested the middleweight titles from him, Len made four successful eleven-stone-six defences, the last of which was against Jack Casey, the 'Sunderland Assassin'. He would have told you that the 'Iron-Man' was his hardest opponent; that punches just bounced off him; that no human fist could ever knock him out.

They enticed Len to Newcastle to meet him and Harvey hit his man with every punch in the book--yet Jack was still in there trying at the final bell. 'He got stronger instead of weaker and I had to fight grimly to stay the fifteen rounds and keep my titles,' Len told me.

Another of the really epic battles of Harvey's career came when, on 7 July '32, he challenged the brilliant French middleweight, Marcel Thil, for his world and European titles in

London, only to be on the wrong end of the decision after fifteen pulsating rounds.

It was midway through 1933 that Harvey moved out of the middleweight picture--and immediately made his mark among the lightheavies and heavyweights. First he outpointed Eddie Phillips to annex the vacant 'cruiser' crown, and at the end of November, he did the same thing to Wales' Jack Petersen to become king of the 'dreadnought' division.

Early the following year he added the Empire heavyweight title to his collection through a win over coloured Larry Gains, but he was deprived of both heavyweight honours, that June, when he gave Petersen a return match. This time Lady Luck was in the Welshman's corner, for in the sixth round a loose lace flicked across Harvey's left eyeball and temporarily blinded him. His eye swelled up enormously and Petersen went all out to win, yet Len's superb defensive ability and clever footwork kept him out of serious trouble.

When a chance blow closed his other eye, he was forced to fight by sheer instinct. Now he was having to listen to the sound of Petersen's boots scraping the ring canvas in order to detect his opponent's whereabouts! In the twelfth round, the referee stopped the fight. Nevertheless, Len had not once been knocked off his feet.

Petersen repeated his win--but this time on points--in January '36 and Len must have regretted his earlier decision, which had meant relinquishing the lightheavyweight title and Lonsdale Belt in order to compete among the big men.

He had, however, taken on added responsibility by becoming matchmaker for Arthur J. Elvin, Managing Director of Wembley Stadium. So, naturally, he was particularly delighted when his new boss agreed to let him match himself against John Henry Lewis for the latter's world twelve-stone seven title in the Empire Pool on 9 November 1936. By now the honour of being British champion at the weight had passed to Eddie Phillips who, by all the rules, should have been given the big opportunity. But any objection to his displacement was silenced by Harvey himself, who pointed out that he had already beaten Phillips at the title weight and that he himself had never lost the championship in the ring.

To save further argument, Len promised to provide Eddie with a shot at the world title in the event of Lewis being defeated, but, for the second time in a world championship bout, he was pipped by a narrow margin. Yet, as against Thil, it was a magnificent failure.

Harvey could also win fights outside the ring. Round about this time he sued a newspaper which had suggested that he had 'pulled his punches' in a contest with a French fighter called Auguste Lengagne. The presiding judge, Mr. Justice McCardie, asked Harvey, when he was in the witness-box, what

was meant by the term 'pulling a punch', and I have it on good authority that Len replied that he had no idea.

'Nonsense', snapped the Judge. 'Come round to me here and aim a blow at my head, but make sure you hold back and do not let it actually land'.

'Shall I be responsible for the consequences, my lord?' asked Harvey. 'I have never done this before; I am used to punching with all the power I possess'.

'In that case, stay where you are', laughed the Judge. It is history that Harvey won his case with costs!

April '38 saw Len conquer his old adversary, Jock McAvoy, to regain the lightheavy title which McAvoy had taken off Eddie Phillips. Eight months later, he beat that same Phillips, on a fourth round disqualification, to capture the national heavyweight crown, of which our Board of Control had deprived Tommy Farr.

Then, the following spring, Harvey added the Empire heavyweight championship to his collection once more by forcing Larry Gains to retire after thirteen rounds. In July '39 he agreed to give McAvoy another crack at the twelve-seven title. The Empire championship, which had been vacant almost twelve years, was thrown in as well. This was the match given recognition in this country as being for the world title, and it was to prove Harvey's last ring outing until he tangled with Mills.

It was the fourth championship meeting between Len and Jock, altogether sixty rounds of grim, gruelling combat. Harvey won on points to make the final tally 3-1 in his favour, and then came a far bigger fight--World War II. Len entered the Royal Air Force as a multi-titleholder, for he now held British and Empire crowns in the two top weight divisions, in addition to his claim to the world twelve-stone-seven diadem.

The truth of the matter is, though, that by the time he fought Mills the latter claim had no real strength. For, in the interim period of three years, no less than seven generally recognised title fights at the poundage had been staged in America.

I shall be filling in Freddie Mills' background in a later chapter, for this is the Len Harvey Story. So, for now, I will do no more than say that, by March '42, Mills had established himself as the legitimate challenger for Harvey's cruiserweight titles. He was then twenty-two years old--an advantage of some twelve years over the champion--and he had finished a loser in only ten out of a total of seventy-three contests.

Freddie was noted for his tremendous strength and outsize fighting heart, rather than for his boxing ability. He was a terrific puncher, especially with the left glove in which he packed a natural and near-perfect left hook.

I was born within half-a-mile of Mills' first home in Bournemouth, and I am sure that no sportswriter can have enjoyed such an early and intimate friendship with Freddie's family. He was my idol and, when I was nine, sixteen-year-old Freddie was just embarking on his ring career. It gives me a bit of a glow to recall that, when Mills first stepped into a boxing ring on the night of 26 March 1936, I made my debut as a ringsider!

Like the champion, the Bournemouthian had enlisted in the RAF soon after war was declared and, a few months before the battle with Harvey, he proudly put up sergeant's stripes. This fact alone made the Harvey-Mills meeting unique, for Len had been granted a Commission in the Service, so that the fight marked the only occasion on record when an Officer and and N.C.O. have contested a professional boxing championship.

Some shrewd judges expressed surprise when Harvey agreed to put his lightheavyweight titles at stake against 'The Mills Bomb '--this nom-de-guerre had become highly popular--on the 'Spurs Football Ground, on 20 June 1942. They thought that, after almost three years of ring idleness, Len would be well advised to retire. I am inclined to think that the champion decided to go through with the Mills match more because he 'felt that he ought to do so,' than from any real desire for further ring combat. I am sure that Harvey realised that, at his age, he could not hope to hit anything like his old form, after such a period of inactivity.

Despite these apparant handicaps, he was known as such a fine ring general that there were many who considered he would still hold too many trump cards for his young challenger.

Immediately after the weigh-in I was with Mills' manager, Ted Broadribb, when a London evening newspaper man approached him and asked his opinion on what pattern the fight would take. Ted's reply left no doubt!

'You can tell your readers that Freddie Mills will win this one very quickly', he said. 'And tell them also that it will probably be all over in the first round'.

Freddie later told me that he and his pilot gained a lot of confidence from meeting Harvey at that weigh-on. Apparently, they spotted that the champion's skin lacked the almost luminous sheen that goes with perfect condition, and this gave the Mills entourage a superiority complex which became even stronger as the Dagenham Girl Pipers piped them down the long aisle and into the ring.

Most of the opening round was spent in cautious exchanges, each man striving to get the measure of his rival. But Harvey's left looked formidable, for with it he seemed capable of keeping Mills at bay with all the ease in the world. As Freddie moved forward, Len would jab and back away until his back was touching the ropes. Then, as Mills began another attack, he would neatly sidestep, leaving the Bournemouthian floundering, and get home with three or four quick, if not damaging, short-arm blows.

Then, with only half-a-minute of the round remaining, I believe that Broadribb decided that Mills would be able to take the hardest blows the champion was capable of throwing without flinching. For he suddenly clapped his hands and yelled: 'Now, Freddie, NOW!'

Like a greyhound out of the trap, Mills shot after his man and the champion, taken aback, was caught by a crushing left hook which shot him across the ring. Before the challenger was able to follow up, the bell rang to end the round.

When Harvey came up for the second round, he had to face all the fury of pulsating youth. The old master found himself pinned on the ropes and a left hook sprawled him on the canvas. He got up at 'eight' to face a killer armed with boxing gloves.

Even Harvey's wonderful defence was unable to withstand the final Mills onslaugh; a terrific smash from the challenger knocked him clean through the ropes on top of the startled scribes in their ringside seats. The referee had called 'out' before Len was able to master his befuddled senses sufficiently to get back into the ring. Mills was the new lightheavyweight kingpin, though Harvey retained his heavyweight laurels, which were not involved.

He never fought again, relinquishing them on his retirement from the sport which he had graced so long and served so well.

Harvey wouldn't talk boxing unless prevailed upon to do so, though I suspect that he relished intelligent discussion about fisticuffs, once motoring down to Bournemouth to aid, by his very presence, a minor tournament I was promoting there. He died in '76 in London.

CHAPTER FIVE: JACKIE PATERSON v. PETER KANE, FOR THE FLYWEIGHT CHAMPIONSHIPS OF THE WORLD, THE BRITISH EMPIRE AND GREAT BRITAIN, AT HAMPDEN PARK, GLASGOW, ON 19 JUNE, 1943.

By 1943 the war had brought professional boxing, let alone big fights, almost to a complete halt. In Great Britain, the Queensberry Club in Soho was the only hall in which regular tournaments were then being staged, but they were of a comparatively minor nature and no championships and scarcely any bouts of national importance were decided there. True, in 1942, an occasional big show had been put on at the Royal Albert Hall, while there was still the odd one at Belle Vue, Manchester and one or two other places. But that was all. The only championship to be decided in 1942 had been that in which, on the Tottenham Hotspur Football Ground, Freddie Mills knocked out Len Harvey to win the lightheavyweight titles. And the only big fight, brief though it was, of 1943 saw Jackie Paterson knock out Peter Kane in Glasgow, while 1944 was to bring only Ronnie James v. Eric Boon at Cardiff and Jack London v. Mills in Manchester.

These were barren times indeed for the grand old sport of fitsicuffs, yet more than a World War would be needed to put boxing on the floor for keeps!

Perhaps, then, it was appropriate that the only really important battle of 1943 involved the Flyweight Championships of Great Britain, the Empire and the World, for had not, at any rate at that time, the eight-stone and under class proved the most satisfactory division of the eight from a British prestige point of view?

I think that in every other class there is heated controversy as to who is the best man ever to have held the world championship, but ask nine fight-fans out of ten who was the greatest flyweight of all time and you will get the same answer--Wales' Jimmy Wilde. I am digressing, of course, because Wilde had his last battle in 1923 but, as a matter of interest, he claimed that, counting his booth career, he had some 850 bouts. It is, however, a matter of fact that he was beaten only four times in some fifteen years of ring warfare.

There was also Glasgow's Benny Lynch. I would add here that many veteran judges rate the Scot above 'The Mighty Atom', because they claim that the tiny Welshman was shrewd enough to 'beat the majority of his rivals on the scales'. That is, they suggest that Jimmy, who thought nothing of giving away stones in weight, often stipulated that his rivals should come in at a poundage less than the one which would allow them to retain their full strength and vitality.

Be that as it may--and as I was not born in the days when Wilde was boxing, I am completely neutral--Lynch really came to the fore in 1935, when he beat Jackie Brown inside two rounds, to capture the British title, and stake a well-founded claim to the world crown. Yet it was not until he outpointed Small Montana in January 1937 that he finally won universal recognition as being world champion.

This fracas was promoted by Sir Arthur Elvin at Wembley, and if anyone had suggested that night that Lynch had only a dozen fights left in his career, and that he was going to lose four of these, that person would have been laughed at as being insane. Yet such was the case, and the first setback came less than six weeks after he had become undisputed world champion. He went to Manchester and was disqualified in the fifth round against Len Hampston. Lynch's seconds jumped in to the ring to save him from what looked like a certain knockout, after he had been floored half-a-dozen times. It was impossible to avoid noticing that Lynch looked only half trained on that occasion--and even that was giving him the benefit of the doubt.

Yet such were the champion's phenonemal powers of recovery that, exactly three weeks later, Lynch went to Hampston's home town of Leeds and handed him a terrific thrashing in ten rounds.

Later he met Peter Kane twice, as we shall see, but from then on all was decline-and-fall for the wee Scot. In June 1938 he was matched to defend the world title against the American Jackie Jurich and, although he won, he had come in pounds overweight and so the world championship had to be declared vacant at the weigh-in. Benny never fought as a flyweight again.

He got licked by a slugger called John Barleycorn, and he finally died as a result of that long and gruelling battle.

When Lynch forfeited his world title, it was agreed that Kane was the leading British contender and that Jurich, who had had a raw deal but was still the leading American challenger, should meet him to stabilize the world title position. Kane won fairly decisively on points. That was in September 1938 and, when war broke out the following year, he joined the Royal Air Force and decided that, for the time being at any rate, he would compete among the bantamweights.

His decision meant that he did not take a crack at the still vacant British title, and with the war less than a month old, Jackie Paterson of Scotland won his nineteenth professional fight and the championship by knocking our Manchester's Paddy Ryan at the Carntyne Dog Track, in Glasgow.

The bout was never particularly memorable, except for the fact that it was the first championship to be staged under real war-time conditions, which made it queer to watch two little men battling away, almost in the shadow of barrage balloons. By the seventh round both Ryan's eyes were cut, and from that time onwards it was merely a question of how long the bout would last. Paterson eventually landed a devastating blow in the thirteenth which put his opponent down and out.

There was no one at home to challenge Paterson seriously at eight stone, and naturally he clamoured for what had now become his rightful shot at the world title. Eventually Kane decided that he would, after all, make a return to the flyweight ranks and he and Paterson were paired to meet for the World, British and Empire championships at Hampden Park, Glasgow, on 19 June 1943. It was to prove one of the shortest title fights on record.

At his best, Kane was a born fighter and the ring held a fascination for him that nothing could alter. As a schoolboy he was happiest when pulling on the gloves and, at the local gymnasium, he was in attendance daily, idolising the professionals and lapping up ring lore as fast as he could assimilate it.

He learned how to punch correctly and where his blows would achieve maximum results, but he never learned the finer points of the Noble Art. Kane was a natural scrapper, and his inborn urge was to keep on attacking until the battle was ended or his opponent had cried 'enough'.

Amateur boxing could not supply sufficient opposition for the Golborne boy. He was now working at the village smithy and daily adding more power to his hitting muscles and building up immense reserves of stamina. He started fighting professionally in Liverpool in 1934, and it was not long before his dynamic punching made him the idol of Merseyside.

He chalked up win after win and, by early 1937, his name was being freely mentioned as a leading contender for Lynch's titles. He was matched to meet the Irishman, Jimmy Warnock, in a final eliminator and, as Warnock had twice beaten the champion in non-title bouts, it looked like being a tough set-to for the 'Golborne Blacksmith'. Yet inside three rounds the Irishman had been punched into a state of utter helplessness!

That win earned Peter a crack at Lynch with the World and British titles at stake, and promoter George Dingley secured the match for Shawfield Park, Glasgow, in October 1937. No flyweight pairing had aroused so much interest in the British Isles since the days of Jimmy Wilde. Everyone recognised in Lynch a champion worthy of the name, a brilliant boxer, cool tactician and deadly puncher. Colourful Kane, on the other hand, was unbeaten in the ring. Entirely without fear, he was a big puncher and possessed supreme confidence in his own ability. He was only nineteen and had been boxing professionally for four years less than the champion. There were 40,000 fans there that night, and what a fight they saw!

In every boxer's career you can usually point a finger at one specific fight and say that this was the highlight of his record. Occasionally two men reach their peak on the same night, and then you see a truly memorable bout. I would say that neither Kane nor Lynch was ever so good again as they were on that October night in Glasgow.

Lynch was perhaps just a shade ahead at the half-way stage, but, at the start of the twelfth, Peter landed one of the hardest blows of the fight, a left hook rather high up on the champion's cheek. As Kane leapt in to follow-up his advantage, Lynch met him with his own perfectly-timed left hook, to the power of which was added the full weight of the challenger as he jumped forward. That was the beginning of the end, and the Golborne youngster was finally counted out in round thirteen.

As a fight, that clash had everything, and it ranks today as one of the finest battles of all time between little men. Peter and Benny met again--on the eve of the 1938 Grand National at Anfield Road Football Ground in Liverpool--but, like so many repeat performances of epic ring battles, this one was only a utility version of the first encounter. It was a non-title affair at catchweights and Lynch, who not for the first time came in at over the agreed poundage, was lucky to be given a draw at the end of twelve rounds.

There followed, for Kane, the Jurich match, shortly after which he was forced to have the little finger of his right hand amputated because of the damage it had suffered in previous fights. It was generally feared that this operation would affect the punching-power that was his main asset, yet he continued undefeated through many more bouts.

While Golborne's world champion was serving in the RAF, he found that he was suffering with eye trouble, and he was told by a specialist that he must never box again. Peter, however, refused to take the doctor's word as final and, after a complicated serious of eye exercises, he eventually overcame the astigmatism which was troubling him.

Jackie Paterson was born in Ayrshire in 1920, but spent some of his early years in the United States of America. As a youth he boxed for the Anderton Amateur Club in Glasgow, and he made his professional debut in 1938. A former shipyard worker Jackie, like Peter, served in the RAF during the war years and, by the time he came up against Kane, he had compiled a fine record at the expense of practically every top-class man of his weight in the country.

Managed by fellow-countryman Pat Collins, Paterson was a 'southpaw' and he packed a terrific dig in either hand which, allied to his not inconsiderable boxing skill, made him a formidable adversary for anyone in the world.

Every time I saw Paterson fight, I was struck by his overall power--not only his punching-power, but also his tremendously thickset build for a flyweight, which made him appear to dwarf his rivals.

After winning the vacant British title in the bout with Paddy Ryan, which I described earlier, he added the Empire crown, which had last been competed for by Elky Clark and George Socks in 1925, by outpointing Kid Tanner of British Guiana at Manchester in March 1940. That was a fine

performance, for, following his arrival in this country, Tanner had proved himself something of a phenomenon by running up some forty consecutive victories. Though the coloured fighter was a natural flyweight, many of these wins were scored over bantam and even featherweights.

And then, in February '41, Paterson gained a second notch on the Lonsdale Belt when he repeated his previous victory over Ryan, only this time the win was scored in the eighth round at Nottingham.

Jackie himself was by no means chary of taking on rivals in a higher weight division, and I well remember him handing out hidings to such as Phil Milligan, Willie Grey, Jimmy Lyden and Canada's Eddie Petrin among the bantamweights; and Ben Duffy, George Pook, Len Davies and Joe Hardy among the feathers. It is a point of interest that, in August '41, he had only gone down by the narrowest of margins when challenging Dundonian Jim Brady for the latter's Empire bantamweight title in Glasgow.

Naturally a colourful ringman, the 'corrie-fisted' Scot (a north-of-the-border term for one who leads with his right hand) always entered the ring wearing red boxing boots to match gaudy red, white and blue shorts.

On that war-time night at Hampden Park, when Kane and Paterson had their brief encounter, there was certainly sensation, even if many of the ringside patrons had scarcely settled in their seats before the main event was all over. For some reason--I

suppose it must have had something to do with war-time restrictions--there only seemed to be one main entrance to the huge arena in use, which meant that it took one the best part of an hour even to get into the ground. Long before the first preliminary pair climbed into the ring, a state of what I can only describe as 'organised chaos' reigned--'organised', I suppose, because there were foot police everywhere, while their mounted counterparts spent the time charging up and down the approaches to Hampden as though they were taking part in a cavalry battle.

Kane was first into the ring, his large Eddie Cantor-like eyes staring as usual. Paterson received the real 'Hampden Roar' of welcome as he made his entry and, though there was little between their respective weights, he certainly looked the bigger man with his thick legs, powerful chest and square shoulders.

A sudden hush descended on the vast stadium as they answered the opening bell. It looked as though Peter intended making the running, for, circling fast to the left away from Paterson's famed left hook, he was the first to lead and seemed to be trying to get to close quarters. Then, as Jackie backed away and threw out a tentative right lead, over came Kane's right. It was a trifle high, and landed on the forehead, yet I believe the Scot was hurt for I saw him blink.

Then, suddenly, before Kane could get back to the onguard position--crash! Paterson fired a left-hook, plumb on

target. Students of the art of boxing will know that the left hook, especially when thrown by a wrong-way-rounder, is the most difficult blow in the book to avoid. It is also the hardest punch to perfect for a man who leads off with his right hand, but Paterson always had this crushing blow as his most powerful asset.

Kane's eyes went glassy, and his legs turned to jelly as he went staggering back into the ropes. The Scot was on him like a flash, raining blows on him from all angles. Paterson was literally keeping the Golborne boy upright by the force of his own blows, as he forced him against the ropes. Gradually, Kane bent double and his knees touched the canvas, then he collapsed. He was out cold, and Paterson had taken just one minute and one second, including the count, to annex the world title and make the Lonsdale Belt his own property.

Scarcely anyone knew it at the time, but Kane had had trouble in making the weight, so that he was but a shadow of his former great flyweight self.

After this lightning victory, Paterson was not called on to defend the world title until the summer of 1946, when he outscored Liverpool's Joe Curran. During the next few years he campaigned as a bantamweight--a division in which he was successful enough to win the British, Empire and European titles in different bouts.

Kane, too, held the European eight-stone-six championship for a spell of some five months between

September '47 and February the following year. Yet he never achieved the same devastating form that he had shown in his heyday as a flyweight.

In the summer of 1947 Paterson was matched, at Glasgow, with Dado Marino from Hawaii, in defence of his world flyweight title. Unfortunately, the bout never materialised. At the weigh-in a message came from the champion stating that he had suffered a nervous collapse. His British, Empire and World titles were subsequently taken from him by the Board of Control.

Later, a match between Marino and Rinty Monaghan was promoted, but Monaghan, who won on points, was not accorded world recognition until he knocked out a ghost-like Paterson in the seventh round at Belfast on 23 March 1948. Jackie had really lost his laurels through making what was now, for him, the impossible poundage of eight-stone.

A few final words to this chapter. We have seen how Lynch, Kane and Paterson each had trouble, as they developed, in coming in at the flyweight limit. I suggest that much of their fighting potential thus became forfeit. To that list can now be added the name of Dai Dower, who was ignominiously humbled by Pascual Perez chiefly on account of being weak at the weight when he took on the world champion. Men of natural eight-stone poundage are becoming fewer and fewer as food and living conditions improve.

Rinty Monaghan and Terry Allen were always genuine flyweights, but neither can be classed as having been a great champion. Jimmy Wilde WAS a great champion but he could not have scaled anywhere near eight-stone, even if he had tried to do so. And that was his good fortune.

CHAPTER SIX: THE LIFE AND DEATH OF DICK CORBETT WHO WAS KILLED DURING THE BLITZ, IN MARCH 1944.

A droning in the night sky mingled eerily with the scuffling of feet in the blackout as the citizens of East London made their way to the Tube Underground Shelter. The beams from the searchlights and the glow from fires lit up the sky to reveal the worried faces of the people, all of whom seemed to be going in the same direction and all of whom seemed bent on getting there first.

That was the trouble, as these folk of all ages, shapes and sizes pushed their way into the narrow entrances of Bethnal Green Underground Station. They had already spent many such nights in the uncomfortable but comparatively safe hideaway, all had had plenty of experience of the horror of air-raids. They were not noticeably frightened, let alone panicky, but when the sirens wailed their warning it was a matter of getting to the shelter quickly, and so being able to claim the more comfortable and roomy positions in which to spend the night.

The warning went as Dick Corbett was on his way home. When he got there, he found the house empty and realised that his wife had taken their children to the nearby Underground for safety.

As he set out to join them there, what can have been his thoughts? Did they perhaps drift back over the wonderful

fighting career that had transformed a frail young cockney into one of Britain's finest bantamweight champions and one whose superb fistic craftsmanship made him a model for the uninitiated? I wonder.

For Dick Corbett, ginger-haired and blue-eyed, was still going strong after more than seventeen years in the ring, and little could he have guessed that he had already fought his last fight.

Anyone who cares to look up Corbett's record will spot straight away that it does not include many knockout victories. On the other hand, though, he gained a surprising number of wins inside the distance, usually on account of the referee stopping those contests when his opponents had dropped hopelessly behind on points.

No, Dick didn't lay any claim to being a KO specialist, for he was no slugger but rather an exponent of pure scientific boxing. It was his straight left, and almost impregnable defence coupled with the complete mastery of the art of in-fighting which enabled him to beat the best. For instance, that brilliant Mancunian fighter, Johnny King, who was a contemporary of Corbett and who met him on no less than five occasions between 1931 and 1935, told me once that boxing with the Bethnal Green man was like trying to nail a ghost.

Corbett was never there when his rivals tried to hit him, King found that the most likely way of registering a hit was to

aim at the body. To throw punches at his head, Johnny said, was quite hopeless unless one had slowed him down first.

At the time I was very young. Johnny, who was staying with my parents, demonstrated his point by placing his hand across the head of an empty lemonade bottle, and then swaying it to-and-fro without moving the base from its original position.

'See how much more the top moves than the bottom', he said. 'It's the same with an elusive fighter like Corbett, for he can sway his head and neck all over the place, but even he can't shift his midriff without moving his feet'. Johnny also pointed out that the midsection provides a much bigger target, and that if one lands a powerful blow to an opponent's body, he will automatically lower his guard momentarily and so provide the chance of a shot at his open chin.

King beat Corbett once by these methods, but Dick scored two points wins over Johnny at Belle Vue, Manchester, and their remaining two bouts finished all square.

Dick was taught to box by his elder brother, Harry, who was a product of the Repton Amateur Boxing Club, which was one of the finest to be found in the East End of London. In those days boys had to fight for very existence in the Bethnal Green area, and if you had fistic aspirations you could only achieve them the hard way. Dick followed in the footsteps of his brother as a member of the club; his father being delighted at the turn of events because young Dick's skinny frame could do with a deal of physical development.

Now, the family name was Coleman, Dick having been christened Richard Truman Ford. He made quick progress as an amateur, and eventually became eager to follow Harry into the paid ranks. Pa Coleman had been against his elder son earning his living by fighting, which was one of the reasons for Harry having adopted the ring-name 'Corbett'. So it was only natural that, when Dick teamed up with his brother in the Ted Broadribb stable, he should take the same ringname.

Harry went on to win the British featherweight title, an honour which he held for just over a year until May 1929. Dick had his first professional contest in 1926, at the age of eighteen, and, though the critics of the time thought a great deal of Harry, that did not stop them sitting up and taking notice when they saw this new Corbett perform.

Within six months Dick took part in fourteen bouts, the following year he went into action twenty-three times, the year after he answered the opening gong on twenty occasions. It will be easily appreciated by those who know their boxing that only a boy who was on the receiving end of far less than any normal boxer's share of punches could hope to stay that pace.

Occasionally Corbett finished on the wrong end of a points decision, but he was never stopped, and it is a fact that throughout his entire career he was never knocked out.

After Harry lost the featherweight title in 1929, the brothers went on a tour of Australia, where both did exceptionally well. Dick won five of his six contests, the remaining one against America's Petey Sarron resulting in a draw. This was in itself a fine performance, when it is taken into account that Sarron was later to win the world featherweight title off Freddie Miller and that Dick was only a bantamweight.

Back home, and Broadribb considered that it was high time his young protege launched an assault on the British eight-stone-six crown. Holder was the renowned Teddy Baldock, and after he had come successfully through a title defence against former champion Alf 'Kid' Pattenden, the newly-formed Board of Control nominated Dick as his official challenger.

But Baldock was having some trouble with his hands, and was not ready to defend his crown. This upset the plans of the National Sporting Club chiefs, who intended staging a mammoth show at Olympia, so instead they brought over the South African, Willie Smith, and matched him with Corbett for the vacant Empire title. Now, in 1927, Smith had trounced Baldock, and he had won the Olympic Games bantamweight championship in Paris back in 1924.

Yet this time Willie met his match, for Dick was in top form and produced a display of boxing that delighted the onlookers. He had the longer reach, and he used this asset to

such good efffect that he completely outfoxed the South African to win comfortably.

Smith wasn't at all satisfied, however, and he complained that the cold English May of 1930 had prevented him being anywhere near his best, challenging Corbett to meet him in a return in South Africa. The Bethnal Green man quite liked the idea, for he was fond of travelling and willingly made the long trip to Johannesburg where he clearly outscored Smith again.

A third meeting between the pair saw Dick lose narrrowly, however. Though in fairness it should be stated that the match was clinched for 'catchweights'--a term meaning above the championship poundage--and that the South African was considerably heavier.

On Corbett's return to London, he found that Baldock was fit again and prepared to meet him--but not in defence of his British championship. Teddy now found it impossible to come in at the bantamweight limit, so he offered to take on Dick at the featherweight poundage of nine stone.

There was not a lot of sense in this arrangement, from the Empire champion's point of view, because he would have little to gain, but much to lose in the matter of prestige, which could so easily affect his drawing-power if he lost.

Yet the whole East End was clamouring, nay yelling, for the match. Baldock had long been their idol, but now Corbett was treading close on his heels. Teddy was the pride of Poplar,

while Dick hailed from the neighbouring borough of Bethnal Green. It was a 'natural' if ever there was one!

Over 30,000 specators were jammed into the Clapton Greyhound Stadium that night, and they were privileged to witness a sparking duel. But the British champion was outspeeded and outboxed by the skilful boy from Bethnal Green, though he did manage to last the distance.

In the early stages of the bout it became obvious to ringsiders that Baldock was but a shadow of the once-great champion who had thrilled them back in the days when Dick Corbett was just a nipper. There were moments, too, when it looked as though Dick could have ended the bout there and then had he been so minded. I like to think that, having taken Teddy's measure, he decided to let the older man go down to graceful defeat in a scientific epic. Indeed, old-timers tell me that Corbett was like that--modest in victory and generous in defeat.

Anyhow, that victory was the turning point of Dick's career. Baldock relinquished the bantamweight title and the Bethnal Green lad was matched with Johnny King for the vacant laurels. Another son of Manchester, Jackie Brown, was the reigning flyweight champion and it was generally expected that King would emulate his fellow-townsman by annexing the bantam crown. Maybe that was because the rainy city had not yet seen Corbett in action!

The Londoner travelled north to meet King at Belle Vue on 21 December 1931, and what a fight the pair put up before a packed house. For fifteen rounds the local man tried to get home his famed right on Corbett's chin, but Johnny just could not land there solidly at all. At the end of a brilliant battle the referee, without hesitation, walked to Corbett's corner and raised his hand in token of victory.

And Dick did not demur at the suggestion of a return, though he must have hoped that it would this time go to some London promoter. But Belle Vue managed to outbid everyone else, so up to Manchester went the Corbetts again, this time to do battle on the 10 October '32 with both of Dick's British and Empire titles at stake.

This was the occasion I mentioned earlier when King concentrated almost exclusively on body punching in the early rounds and so succeeded in slowing-down the Londoner. Having done so, he adopted tactics completely foreign to him and left-handed his way to victory. So busy was Corbett watching out for the Mancunian's dynamic right and so much had King's earlier body-punching taken out of him, that he allowed himself to be outscored in a battle of left hands for about the only time in his life.

'You sneaked the verdict off me', Dick told the northerner afterwards, 'but you'll never lick me again as long as you live!'

Well, they had three more set-tos' and Corbett lived up to his prophecy, though he twice had to be content with a share of the honours. Sixteen months later he smothered King's body-punching to regain his titles--once again in King's home town--and then the pair boxed a draw in London during August '34. But his efforts to make the required weight had sapped Dick's strength!

Now, in order to win a Lonsdale Belt outright, one has to win three fights involving the British championship at any one weight. As Dick had already won two and drawn one, it meant just one more win in a title match and the gold bantamweight belt would be his for keeps. And he was sure that he could always beat King who, as a result of their most recent clash, was still the outstanding contender. So naturally Corbett's heart was set on it.

Once more the fight went to Manchester, but again the Bethnal Green boxer had to wage war with the scales. When he arrived at the weigh-in he was two pounds overweight, so he lost his titles on the scales and the fight went on at 'catchweights'.

It was a bitter blow for Corbett--and a very costly business. His cut of the purse should have been £450, but out of that he had to pay £200 weight forfeit and and additional £100 for breaking his contract. Thus he received only £150 for the fifteen rounds that again ended in a draw.

After this his only alternative was to compete in the featherweight class, and Dick proved that the change was for the best. He won fourteen bouts in a row against the best in the country and, by the early part of 1936, found himself matched with the Scot, Johnny McGrory, in a final eliminator for Nel Tarleton's British title.

Sad to relate, all the breaks went against him. During training he complained of pains in his back, but he would not hear of a postponement. He was in such pain while actually fighting that McGrory romped home a good winner. Afterwards the doctor's examination disclosed a fractured vertebrae leading to the liver, and Dick was kept in plaster of paris for six weeks or more.

Despite Corbett's tremendous handicap, it was only in the later stages of the twelve-rounder that McGrory really managed to get on top. At the start, the Londoner took command of the centre of the ring, and forced McGrory to circle around him and make all the running. Dick's plan was to rely on counter-punching, for he knew that if he could make his opponent continually move towards him, he would not have to throw his own blows so far, and could minimise the awful pain which nagged him with practically every movement he made.

It was a tribute to his wonderful ringcraft that Dick did this successfully for the opening four rounds. But the Scot was no slouch in the matter of boxing ability and, when he realised

the Corbett plan was to make him lead, he feinted cleverly and so worked openings which he was quick to exploit. Corbett must have been thankful to hear the final bell, but he was not disheartened, for, if he had been able to acquit himself so creditably against McGrory when boxing under the burden of a serious handicap, what might he be able to do when fully fit?

Sure enough, once he was fit again, Dick set about chasing the Scot (who had in the meantime relieved Tarleton of the title) and he subsequently tried in vain to get Johnny's three successors as champion into the ring. These were 'Spider' Jim Kelly, Johnny Cusick and Tarleton--who regained his laurels in February 1940.

But though, from the time he abandoned the bantamweight division, to the outbreak of war Corbett lost only four out of forty contests, his setbacks came at the wrong moments and he never got another crack at the championship.

When war was declared in September '39 Dick was one of the first to enlist, but his service in the Forces was short-lived, for the doctors soon discovered that he suffered from an ear defect and this caused him to be discharged. So instead he joined Civil Defence, where he put in sterling work for nearly four years.

Boxing tournaments in those dark days were practically non-existent, but in late 1943 a show in aid of War Charities was staged at Shepherd's Bush. Dick, always ready to help a good cause, was paired in a ten-rounder with a leading Scottish featherweight named James Watson and was adjudged the loser on points. It was his last fight.

For it was on the night of 3 March 1944 that Corbett set out to meet his wife and family in the Bethnal Green Underground shelter. When he got there the East End folk were flocking down the stairs in their hundreds. As a Civil Defence volunteer, well-known to the locals, Corbett did his best to keep some semblance of order among the throng.

Suddenly a bomb went off with a blinding flash and deafening explosion in the immediate vicinity of the shelter, and the hitherto orderly procession was straightaway transformed into the mad stampede of a panicky mob, intent only on getting to safety underground.

The boxer was on the stairs when he saw a young mother, carrying a baby, trip and fall. Dick snatched up the child and vainly tried to check the oncoming people while the mother regained her feet.

But the sudden surge forward was quite uncontrollable, for those in the rear were pushing those in front of them clean off their feet, and the place was just an avalanche of bodies.

Scores of people were crushed to death or suffocated, while many more were injured. When the awful mass was finally removed, Corbett's body was the very last to be recovered. He

was dead, but, beneath his body and clutched tightly in his arms, was the baby--miraculously still alive.

Dick had lived round there and had fought round there. And that was where he died..

CHAPTER SEVEN: NEL TARLETON V. AL PHILLIPS, FOR THE BRITISH AND EMPIRE FEATHERWEIGHT CHAMPIONSHIPS AT BELLE VUE, MANCHESTER, ON 23 FEBRUARY, 1945.

When Nel Tarleton's hand was raised in victory by referee Ben Hardwicke after fifteen gruelling rounds against London's Al Phillips at Belle Vue, Manchester, on 23 February 1945, he became the first fighter to win two Lonsdale Belts outright, though the feat has since been accomplished by several others.

And, though 'Peerless' Jim Driscoll must be ranked as the greatest of all British featherweights, 'Nella' from Liverpool is a good second, even though he could never lay claim to the world championship. Both Driscoll and he started in their 'teens and fought on until the age of forty, and neither was ever knocked out, while both retired as undefeated champion. Tarleton it was who twice recaptured the title after losing it in the ring, to put a spoke in the adage that 'They Never Come Back'.

Nel had two shots at the world title, losing on both occasions to the brilliant 'southpaw' American, Freddie Miller. He won the Empire crown in 1940, yet never fought for European honours. He also licked the terrific-punching British lightweight champion, Al Foreman, in a non-title bout and boxed a draw with 'Panama' Al Brown, who was at that time world bantamweight champion.

Though he was in action from 1926 right up to 1945--the defence of his British and Empire titles against Phillips was his final ring outing--Tarleton was never once beaten inside the distance, which clearly demonstrates the type of boxer he was. He was super-scientific. He had to be, for he was far from being tough and rugged, being built on rather delicate lines and standing very tall for his weight. Brilliant left hand work, combined with an abnormally long reach stood him in good stead, despite poor health right from his early days in schoolboy boxing yet, before his twentieth birthday, he decided to turn professional.

Soon he was a favourite at the old Liverpool Stadium in Pudsey Sreet, his christian name of Nelson being reduced to 'Nel' in order the better to fit advertising posters. Then a bantamweight, he was soon taking part in fifteen-rounders against some of the top men in the country.

After a long run of successes in Liverpool, he met bantamweight kingpin Johnny Brown at Premierland, London. Tarleton lost, but, soon afterwards, he outpointed one of the recognised contenders for the featherweight title, Billy Hindley, at the National Sporting Club. He now decided to move up a division and campaign among the nine-stone men. A few months later at Liverpool, he took the Northern Area title off Dom Volante, who was another of the recognised contenders for the national crown.

Though he was now a top-liner, the way was not clear for a crack at the British title despite the fact that 'Nella', as he had come to be affectionately known by this time, had chalked up thirty-three successive wins since the defeat by Brown. So, in 1929, he visited America where he had eight fights, winning all but two. The Americans did not enthuse over the pale-faced Britisher, so Tarleton returned home to oppose Johnny Cuthbert for the featherweight crown at Liverpool in early November, 1930. The result of this essay into a championship boxing was a draw which meant that Cuthbert retained his laurels, but, some eleven months later, Nel got a return match on the Anfield Football Ground,. This time, he proved himself the superior boxer to win on points.

Thirty-thousand fans saw his brilliant victory, gained almost exclusively by left hand work. It transpired later that the Liverpudlian had badly damaged his right early in the bout.

Nine bouts and thirteen months went by and then, to the amazement of his supporters and to Nel's own surprise, Seaman Tommy Watson, a 'Geordie', deprived him of his coveted crown. To make matters worse, Watson did the deed right in Nel's own backyard of Liverpool! The loss of his Belt and title put a stop to Tarleton's plans for a second trip to the United States, but, in the summer of 1933, he went 'down-under' to Australia, for a series of matches, taking brother-in-law Ernie Roderick with him. Tarleton broke even in three contests, winning, drawing and

being outscored in turn. Both he and Roderick found the climate trying, and they were glad to get home again.

Watson gave him a return title fight in July '34 and this time the Lonsdale Belt, which, of course, goes with the British title, returned to the Liverpudlian. Later that year Freddie Miller, who as a visiting world champion was on a barn-storming tour of this country, defended his world title against Nel, and got home only by what must have been the narrowest of margins. Two weeks before Christmas, however, Tarleton met Dave Crowley at the Empire Pool, Wembley, and gave the capacity crowd a delightful exhibition of the arts and crafts of boxing, to win his first Lonsdale Belt outright.

To accomplish this feat, one needs three wins in title bouts, but not necessarily successive ones.

The next two years saw him as busily engaged as ever. In June 1935 he had another world title bout with Miller, only to lose again on points. Another six engagements followed, then a title defence gainst bantamweight champion Johnny King from Manchester. Nella won by a handsome margin of points, but as the National Sporting Club had stopped issuing Belts, he had to wait a further four months before the British Boxing Board of Control--this body had come into being in 1929--put up a new trophy for the nine-stone division and nominated Johnny McGrory to contest its ownership with Tarleton.

McGrory was a clever and hard-working young Scot and he caused something of a surprise by getting home on points. Nel was disappointed with his performance and he went into 'semi-retirement', eventually engaging in two bouts after a five-month layoff. Then he rested for another eight months. From this time on he made only spasmodic appearances in the ring until 1940, when the late Johnny Best senior, first gentleman of boxing and promoter at Liverpool Stadium, made him a good offer to meet Johnny Cusick who, the previous June, had taken both the British and Empire titles off 'Spider' Jim Kelly in Belfast.

Naturally Tarleton was delighted at this chance of regaining the British title, and he must also have been influenced by the fact that the Empire crown would also be at stake. Anyhow, Nel rose to his task magnificently and he well won on points. In November '40 the Liverpudlian gained a second notch on that second Belt, when he proved too clever for Sunderland's Tom Smith, who was the only top--class boxer I ever knew to be brought to the fore by a Roman Catholic priest.

During the next four years Nella had a total of only fourteen contests--one of which was a points reverse at the hand of that same Tom Smith. But both boxers' Service commitments prevented them being brought together again in a title match.

This, then, was the champion who first won his British crown in 1931 and, on 23 February 1945, was still fighting in defence of that title, besides having, in 1940, added the Empire

championship to it. Now he only needed just one more successful defence to make a second Belt his own property, for there had been no Belt at stake for that 1936 title win over King. But, besides having engaged in numerous fights over those years, Nel had also undergone an attack of pneumonia, a severe road accident, innumerable bouts of pleurisy, and had only recently discovered that one of his lungs had been defective all his life.

His challenger was Al Phillips of Aldgate, London, known as 'The Aldgate Tiger', because of the ferocious way in which he set about his opponents. Phillips was the champion's junior by fourteen years, and he did not begin his ring career until 1939. A Jewish fighter, he was no stylist but rather one whose savage attack clubbed down all the opposition that stood between him and a crack at the title. He was also exceedingly durable, packed a hefty dig in either glove and seemed likely to prove too strong for thirty-nine-yearold Nel.

One of a family of seven brothers and two sisters, he had done quite well as an amateur boxer and served in the Royal Navy during the war. Quite soon he had been shore-based at Liverpool and Johnny Best gave him some of his first professional bouts at the Stadium and at another of his venues in Blackpool.

In 1942 Aldgate Al won six fights in succession in London and, the following year, I saw him fight often in Old

Compton Street, Soho, at what was then the Queensbury Club and later the London Casino. And it was there that he really began to make a name for himself.

He was soon included in a series of eliminators for the purpose of finding a challenger for Tarleton. In these, he first beat Jim Brady on points, then annihilated Torquay's George Pook inside a round and, in the final, overcame Len Davies of Wales, who was disqualified in the sixth round for holding persistently in his efforts to avoid Phillips' non-stop flow of hooks and swings.

Both Phillips and Tarleton had tremendous personal followings, so that there was hectic bidding between London, Liverpool and Manchester to secure the title-fight. As Belle Vue emerged victorious in the 'battle of the bids', several hundred of Al's supporters made the journey north from London. But the Manchester stadium accommodates somewhere in the region of 7,000 spectators, and I am sure that all the northerners there were bent on seeing 'Old Nella' give his youthful challenger a boxing lesson.

The champion was serving in the Royal Air Force at this time, but he was fortunate enough to be on a station where he was given every facility to train for the fight and he had the services of several first-class sparring-partners.

The Aldgate man trained at the then well-known basement gymnasium in Fitzroy Square, near Warren Street

Undergound Statin, and he impressed the critics, most of whom thought that the veteran champion would be unable to hold tearaway Al off for the the long fifteen-round journey. Therefore, they mostly tipped Phillips to become the new champion, seemingly secure in the knowledge that Tarleton did not carry a sufficiently heavy punch to bring him victory inside the distance.

As was expected, the challenger stormed into aged Nel from the opening gong and gave him no rest. Relying almost exclusively upon swinging punches from either hand, the Londoner gained scant succcess at the outset, for Tarleton, poised high on his toes, boxed carefully and made full use of his long left arm. He would block, duck and slip Phillips' blows all the while. Al kept trying to bully him out of his stride, but ringwise Nel looked to hold all the aces. With consummate artistry he would tie his challenger up in the clinches, or leave him floundering on the ropes, and back-pedal with quiet confidence, drawing Phillips on to occasionally disconcert the Londoner with a quick flurry of blows.

Then, in the fifth round, we had a glimpse of the drama that was to follow. One of Phillips' right swings connected solidly and the champion lurched back into the ropes. Al rained blow after blow on him as he swayed, apparently groggily, first this way then that. Yet Al could not nail him and he must have been, at any rate partially, foxing. Because all of a sudden the old

master was back in the centre of the ring and launching an attack of his own.

The sixth went to Tarleton, the seventh to Phillips. The eighth I would say, was even, for, though several swings reached the champion's head, he was always riding them when they arrived and Al himself had to take a goodly number of counter-punches from his taller opponent.

Sensation came in the tenth. The challenger, as he had done countless times before, threw a full-blooded right at Nella's chin and, for once, the champion was a trifle slow to see it coming. Tarleton's eyes glazed and his knees sagged and Phillips belaboured Nella as a cat would a mouse. Four more heavy rights and a smashing left swing landed smack on his jaw before he was able to set up a cross-armed, protective cover. It looked as though he must go down--that he did not do so was due, on his own admission afterwards, to the fact that he was just able to realise in the midst of that storm, that if he once went to the canvas his fast-failing strength would almost certainly prohibit his rising again. Therefore gallant Nel propped himself against the ropes to meet the full force of that onslaught. It seemed impossible that the veteran champion could last the round, but he did just that...

Round eleven was rather an anti-climax, and I remember thinking that Phillips had probably lost heart through his inability to finish Nella off in the preceding session. He still

chased, but he was much slower now and, in the twelfth, Tarleton cut out just as much of the leading as did his younger rival.

It was in that round that serious misfortune struck the challenger. He took a right to the chin from Tarleton, and was suddenly limping and shaking his right leg, the victim of a painful attack of cramp. Like the old ring general he was, the Liverpudlian immediately took over the role of aggressor and Phillips was punched round the ring until the gong. He was unable to make any impression on the now super-confident champion in the three rounds that remained, never completely recovering his aggressive poise.

At the final bell the men were locked in a clinch, with the Londoner still obviously in pain. As referee Hardwicke lifted his hand in token of victory, hordes of Nella's supporters invaded the ring, to carry him shoulder high back to his dressing-room.

Nel Tarleton had won his second Lonsdale Belt outright and, having made his son Brian a present of the first, he now announced that he had promised his twin daughter, Sandra, that he would give her the second trophy, should he win it.

On the afternoon of the fight I heard it whispered over tea in Manchester's Midland Hotel that Phillips had been troubled with cramp while in training. After the final bout of the evening that night at Belle Vue I spoke to Tarleton--spick and span in his RAF uniform--as he and his entourage left the arena. Nel

remarked that he was sorry Al had been handicapped, but that, in his opinion, it was the right-hand blow with which he had struck his rival that had been the cause of the damage.

'I think that punch upset a nerve centre in Al's leg', he said. Then, referring to brother-in-law Ernie Roderick, he added: 'Ernie once did the same kind of thing against a Continental opponent. He knocked him down for the full count, and then, when he had seemingly recovered, his rival had to be assisted from the ring because he was in pain, having developed a similar kind of limp'.

Coming from the opposition camp, as it did, that is merely an opinion--one with which, bearing in mind what I had heard at the hotel the same afternoon, I am not inclined to agree.

Shortly after this fine battle, Tarleton announced his retirement. Apparently, he had underaken a special tryout in his private gymnasium, and decided that his legs would no longer stand up to the strain of fifteen-three-minute rounds. I must, in fairness, state that that fact alone makes me wonder what might have occurred in those final three rounds, had Phillips not met misfortune in the twelfth.

Both of Tarleton's titles, of course, became vacant on his retirment. In March 1947 Phillips annexed the Empire crown when he outpointed coloured Cliff Anderson from British Guiana. Two months later, he added the European championship, when overcoming that brilliant French scrapper, Raymond Famechon.

But in September the same year he dropped a verdict to Blackpool's Ronnie Clayton in a three-championship battle which included the still vacant British title. This setback meant that Al from Aldgate was no longer a champion, and that he was not to hold a Lonsdale Belt. It marked the end of his championship career.

Sad to relate that Tarleton, never strong and consistently dogged throughout his life by ill-health, was rushed to hospital, early in 1956, where he underwent a major operation. Although he was released to go home, it was an open secret among his friends that Nella could not last very long. The only time I saw him again, I noticed that he looked pallid and drawn, and he died a few days before his fiftieth birthday, which would have been on l4 February 1956.

He was, perhaps, the finest scientific scrapper that I ever saw.

CHAPTER EIGHT: GUS LESNEVICH V. FREDDIE MILLS, FOR THE LIGHTHEAVYWEIGHT CHAMPIONSHIP OF THE WORLD, AT HARRINGAY ARENA ON 14 MAY, 1946.

There are instances when a change of management marks a change in a boxer's fortunes. Two such examples stick out in my mind particularly, because the same manager was responsible in both instances. It was Ted Broadribb, himself formerly a first-rate fighter, who was the dominant factor in the rise of both Tommy Farr and Freddie Mills, two men who might never have scaled the heights or boxed for world's championships had it not been for his arrival on the scene. Both Farr and Mills had been boxing for a number of years before he took them in hand, and, from that moment onwards, they were placed on the path to the top.

Of all places, the seaside resort of Bournemouth is about the last place one would earmark as the birthplace of a world-beating prize-fighter. Yet Freddie Mills was born there on 26 June 1919 and he might never have given professional boxing a thought had it not been for the fact that promoter Jack Turner commenced fortnightly shows at the local Ice Rink. By the time Mills was sixteen, boxing in Bournemouth was firmly established, and so it was only natural that a bright-eyed youngster should be attracted to the sport. Besides this, Freddie's elder brother, Charlie, was already fighting professionally and it was not long before Frederick Percival followed his example. After winning a novices' competition, Mills began to follow the booths attached to the travelling fairs, matching his youth and strength against the hard-bitten booth ringsters.

When the fair business broke up at the end of the autumn, Freddie returned to Bournemouth and found plenty of work with Jack Turner, who brought the best of the London and provincial middleweights to meet his find. The majority returned home, well beaten.

At the outbreak of war Freddie joined the R.A.F., but he still managed to secure a fight or two in provincial towns and, on one occasion, outpointed the champion, Jock McAvoy, in Liverpool. His old manager, Bob Turner, also enlisted and Mills was taken in hand by Ted Broadribb. In his first London appearance he stopped Tommy Martin in five rounds, but he was now a fully-fledged lightheavyweight who was quite prepared to meet heavyweights as well in order to keep busy.

Meeting McAvoy in a return engagement--this time it was officially labelled as a final eliminator for Len Harvey's lightheavyweight titles--Freddie practically paralysed his rival with his first big punch, to win in the opening round, and then he knocked out Len Harvey in two rounds, to become British and Empire champion at twelve-stone-seven.

But this was 1942 and there was still a war on. For two years Mills had to be content with the boxing he could get as a physical-training instructor then, in September 1944, he lost by a very close margin of points in a bout against sixteen-stone Jack London for the vacant British and Empire heavyweight championships. After stopping Scottish champion Ken Shaw, five months later, he was posted to India where he remained until the spring of 1946. He had been out of action for the best part of a year, serving in a country where the climate is detrimental to an athlete, yet this amazing fellow came home and, with only the shortest of preparations, took part in a world title contest.

About this time Jack Solomons had established himself as the leading promoter in the country. He had obtained the rights to promote at Harringay and wanted a really big fight to top his opening bill there. He flew to America and succeeded in signing Gus Lesnevich, as world lightheavyweight kingpin, to meet the new British heavyweight champion, Bruce Woodcock, in a catchweights contest which would, of course, not have involved Lesnevich's world title. But a snag arose as far as Woodcock was concerned, and the match had to be called off.

Therefore, Solomons was particularly delighted when Mills arrived at his office one day, to announce that he was home again and just itching for action. Would he meet Lesnevich in place of Woodcock? Yes, if it was for the world championship.

'I'll get Gus to agree to defend the title here, whatever it costs, and you'll get your big chance on May l4', promised Solomons. Eventually the American's camp accepted the London promoter's proposal, but he had to agree to Lesnevich's demand for a £12,000 purse.

Gus and his manager, Joe Vella, arrived to make themselves a hightly popular pair. The American was more than four years Mills' senior, which made him on the wrong side of thirty-one. On the other hand, he was far more experienced than the British champion, though Freddie had himself been in the game for ten years. As an amateur, Lesnevich had won the Golden Gloves competition at middleweight then, for two years, he fought the best of the professionals, eventually making a trip to Australia, where he was a great success.

By the time he reached home Gus was a lightheavyweight. Billy Conn had just annexed the world championship--it was now 1939--and the pair were matched. Lesnevich was outscored, after a terrific struggle, and they met again, nine months later, with Billy again just about good for his win. Soon Conn decided to compete as a heavy and Gus beat Antoine Christoforidis to win the crown. He twice defended his laurels against Tami Mauriello, and then he joined the U.S. Coastguard Services. At the end of 1945, he was honourably discharged and resumed his boxing career with a one-round knockout victory over Joe Kahut. He only took part in one other contest, and that a non-title outing, before meeting Mills, so it can be seen that, if the Britisher was short of ring practice, so was the world champion.

It looked a marvellous match, and a fortnight before the date of the fight all tickets had been sold. Considering that ringside tickets were priced as high as twenty guineas, this was really something. And I well recall how, on the night, I saw a late purchaser pay £75 for one of these from a 'tout' outside the stadium!

Harringay Arena was packed to the rafters when Lesnevich and Mills took the ring. The visitor was warmly welcomed by the 11,000-odd crowd, but the cheers that greeted Freddie fairly shook the building. Never had I known such a tense atmosphere at a boxing match when referee Eugene Henderson issued his final instructions. I know that, at the opening bell, my throat was dry and my heart was in my mouth. After the long years of blackouts and wartime crowd restrictions, this was indeed an occasion to remember. They truly came out fighting.

Mills walked straight in, swinging his famed left hook. But he was brought up short by Gus' straight left leads, while he rolled those bull-like shoulders of his. Then the challenger worked his way to close quarters only to let rip left swings that missed and a right chop that hit thin air. Suddenly, that left hook of Freddie's caught Gus off balance, and the American back-pedalled swiftly before the Bournemouth battler could crowd in and really go to work. The bell.

Mills tore from his corner at the start of the second in an obvious attempt to pin Gus down before he had a chance to take command of the centre of the ring. Lesnevich met him coolly and, instead of using the fancy footwork that would take him clear of the rush, the world champion shot out a straight left that brought Freddie up sharp. Then, before Mills could take any evasive action, his rival crashed over a right to the chin and the Britisher went down for a count of 'six'. With cat-like speed, Gus crossed the ring as he rose and hit him again.

Nobody expected Mills to beat the count after that blow, for it had again been a perfectly-timed right to the jaw, delivered with every ounce of Lesnevich's weight behind it. But he made it, struggling to his feet in an obvious daze. Amid the uproar, the count was inaudible, and only the timekeeper could have known exactly how many seconds Mills was actually on the canvas.

A brilliant combination of punches again slumped Freddie to the boards, and it is one of the miracles of his career--indeed, of ring history--that he managed to rise in time, yet again. Further severe punishment followed and, when they got him back to his corner after that sensational round, even his most ardent supporters were praying that his handlers would persuade him to stay there. We loved him as a fighter, but we loved him even better as a person. No one wanted to see him take any more punishment.

Yet he proceeded to perform a second miracle, for, filling up that deep chest of his, Mills came up for the third with chin tucked well down into his massive left shoulder and walked right into the surprised American to batter him two-handed all round the ring.

The cheering was deafening as Freddie brought the blood gushing from Lesnevich's left eye and nose. It was a worried Gus who returned to his corner at the end of the round, and a positively distressed one who completed the fourth and fifth. Mills, calling on some incredible reserve of stamina and making full use of his amazing powers of recuperation, had resorted to brilliant left-hand boxing to stem the tide.

Midway through the contest, he brought his chopping right hand back into play to smash the American's nose. Lesnevich now had to fight with his mouth open in order to get the air through to his lungs and, in addition, his left eye was almost completely closed. Gus presented a fearful picture, yet all the time his left was tattooing Mills' ribs and face.

I was sitting behind the American's corner, and as he returned to his stool at the end of the ninth, I saw him shake his head in dejection at his manager, Joe Vella. I thought it was all over and that a new champion had been crowned. But evidently Benny Huntman, who was acting as Lesnevich's chief second, pleaded with Vella to be allowed to patch the injury up for just one more effort. That he did indeed do so is now history.

Critics would tell you that, in the next round--the fatal tenth--Mills got careless through over-confidence. But it is my firm conviction that, since going down for the second time during the second round, he had been boxing in a complete daze and purely by instinct. Now, I think, full consciousness was returning and with it the bewilderment of his surroundings.

At any rate, he left his corner far more slowly than before, hands low and feet seemingly glued to the canvas. When he swung a left, Freddie missed and, in an instant, Lesnevich had jumped in to land a cracking right to the point.

Mills hit the deck but just succeeded in rising in time. Another blow dropped him again and, midst a shocked silence, the courageous British champion struggled up again. A desperately vicious Lesnevich awaited him. Down went Freddie again, and it was while he was on the floor that Eugene Henderson lifted the American's hand to signify his retention of the title.

Ignoring the hot controversy on the subject of Henderson's action which followed, it is fact that when the referee intervened, the time-keeper's watch indicated that there were only four seconds of the round remaining--insufficient for the British champion to have been counted out! And, bearing in mind his miraculous recovery during the interval between the second and third rounds, might he not have been able to do a repeat performance?

If the owners of Harringay had wanted something really spectacular to put the arena once more in the public spotlight as a boxing venue, Mills and Lesnevich certainly provided that very thing. For today that fight is still talked about as one of the greatest mauls ever witnessed in London,. It has been the subject of more controversy, too, than any other battle between big men.

Was the referee right or wrong? That has been the question asked in boxing circles ever since. I think that the referee's action was warranted, for he could not possibly have known that so few seconds of the round remained and the punishment that the Bournemouth fighter had absorbed was, in my opinion, quite sufficient to justify calling a halt. I think that it was the current fortunes of the contest that aroused so much adverse comment. For Mills appeared, after his appalling start, to have got on top and, indeed, only to have had to hold on to become world champion.

Yet there can be little doubt that the British champion undertook that fight too soon after returning home from India, where his blood had been thinned by the conditions. Also that he was not sufficiently re-acclimatised to the rigours of the English climate.

I firmly believe that Mills lost that fight through leaving his first world-title chance in the rings of South-East Asia, where he and the Leeds heavyweight, Al Robinson, did so much to

entertain the troops. That night at Harringay he still began by throwing over-hand rights which were really his own undoing.

In those exhibitions he used to try to demonstrate how he had knocked out Robinson in an actual contest they had had before going overseas. He would throw an overhand right to Robinson, a much taller man than himself, prepared for it to be blocked before getting in a finishing left hook. Against a boxer of Gus' capabilities, that was just not good enough.

Many people called that overhand right of Freddie's his 'Hammer and Nails' punch, which describes it fairly accurately. It was only after those second round counts that he forgot all about it and, under the influence of the blows he received, boxed naturally.

Ted Broadribb once told me that he felt that both Freddie and he owed their thanks to referee Henderson. If he had not stopped the fight at the moment he did, Mills might never have been in a position finally to dethrone Lesnevich in a return meeting, which he did in July 1948 at London's White City.

In addition, Ted told my father, a close friend of his, of how grey and ill Freddie looked as they left the arena. On the way home, Broadribb had to stop the car on a number of occasions for Mills to vomit. 'In the end he was vomiting nothing', said Ted, 'and I was very worried'. Yet perhaps it was just as well, for there is no more efficient safety valve for concussion, and there can be little doubt that the British champion was severely concussed for

several days afterwards. Freddie later revealed that, in his opinion, he was never quite the same fighter after the terrific pummelling he took in that first great battle with Gus Lesnevich, despite the fact that he was able to conquer his old rival at the second attempt.

For a whole week subsequent to that terrific fight his speech was slurred at odd times and every morning he had to be woken up from a deep sleep which was more like a coma than anything else. He also suffered from an almost continuous headache.

The fact is that, on that May day in 1946, Messrs. Mills and Lesnevich put up the greatest fight seen in this country for a very long time. My own belief is that Gus, too, never quite achieved the same fistic greatness again that he attained on that epic occasion, for this was a battle in which courage and gameness in unlimited quantities were on display for all to see.

It was a world championship clash of the highest possible order and I, for one, always get a thrill when I recall it and a kick out of being able to say: 'I WAS THERE!'

CHAPTER NINE: BRUCE WOODCOCK V. JOE BAKSI, TEN ROUNDS INTERNATIONAL HEAVYWEIGHT CONTEST AT HARRINGAY ARENA ON 15 APRIL, 1947.

I should think that several miles of newsprint have been filled on and about heavyweights, for the dreadnoughts of boxing have a certain something entirely their own and which no other weight in the sport can command. Of those miles, Bruce Woodcock of Doncaster once claimed his fair share of comment and thick headlines--perhaps more than most, for he came into the picture when Britain was sadly impoverished in the 'big-men' category. With Jack Solomons already operating in the American fistic territory, as a nation we felt honour bound to find a man ready and competent to do battle with the best importations from the States.

It was considered that we had him in the person of Woodcock, for, from January 1942, when he first swopped cutlery for cash, his record read undefeated until May of 1946, when he made a trip to America to tangle with Tami Mauriello and sufffered a fifth-round knockout.

But after this setback he went on to collect another two fistic scalps in the persons of Freddie Mills and Al Renet (from whom he won the European championship). Yet still the big question remained--could our heavyweight champion hold his own with a top American?

It was natural then, that when Woodcock faced Gus Lesnevich, America's World Lightheavyweight Champion, at Harringay on 17 September 1946, the place was packed. Lesnevich had, as I have described in another chapter, previously trounced Mills, and his fighting qualities were known and appreciated in England. In the minds of everyone this was testing time for Bruce, and he knocked the American out in the eighth round, though, in my book, he was behind on points at the time and that with only two full rounds to come.

Yet the Doncaster man showed up well. He was cool, even when sadly perplexed by the ring generalship and accurate punching of Lesnevich. And the punch that smacked Gus down to be counted out I am sure would have dropped any other man for keeps. It was a match-winning blow all the way; a full-blooded right to the jaw.

A word here about Woodcock's punching. In my opinion the Doncastrian was one of the few big men who hit correctly. He held his hands correctly and he delivered his blows with the knuckle part of the glove. He also punched his full weight and, whatever faults he may be said to have had, one of them was not that of incorrect punching.

Bruce had two other fights before the end of 1946, stopping Frenchman Georges Martin in seven rounds at Belle Vue, Manchester, in November and then licking Nisse Andersson,

a huge Swede, in three rounds at Harringay just a week before Christmas.

Now to 1947. Joe Baksi, big, solid, heavy-punching ex-miner of Czechoslovak stock, had come over from the States the previous November, to force Freddie Mills to retire after the sixth round of their Gay Fawkes night bout at Harringay.

Promoter Solomons, looking round for a top-liner for the big show he was planning for the same arena on 15 April 1947, suggested that Woodcock might like the chance to go in with the big Yankee. 'After all', he said to Tom Hurst, the British champion's manager, 'Baksi is rated high in the States and, if Woodcock beats him, he will certainly have wiped out any suggestion of lost prestige from his setback against Mauriello'.

As part of Bruce's tuning-up programme, it was agreed that he should take part in one serious fight first. It turned out to be against Stephan Olek, a Polish-born Frenchman, at Belle Vue four weeks before the big fight. As Woodcock's European title was at stake, the bout was a fifteen-rounder and, though Bruce won clearly enough, the set-to went the full distance. This did not please the critics, but Olek was a cagey and ringwise performer and, in any case, I know that Woodcock was still suffering the effects of an attack of 'flu.

So to the Baksi match, which marked one of the most tragic episodes in the long and disappointing history of British heavyweight boxing. Joe himself was a strange mixture of

childishness and brutality. He loved practical joking, but, on his night, he could be ruthless in the ring and fight with great viciousness. He had clashed with most of the leading heavyweights in the States and it was generally conceded that, at his best, he was more than a match for the challengers to world champion Joe Louis.

The fight, I think, was the most brutal I have ever watched. I was extremely fortunate to be there at all, for I had only recently begun National Service in the Army. It was only because the Physical Training Instructor in the unit was a fight-fan and so was making the trip to Harringay himself, that I was able to make use of my own 'brief'. By coincidence, it also happened to be my twenty-first birthday!

I am sure that all England wanted Woodcock to win that night. After all, a British boy was battling on the threshold of boxing's house of highest honour, the house wherein dwells the Heavyweight Champion of the World. We all wanted him to gain admission.

When the bell sounded for the start of the fight, Bruce's jerky movements made it obvious that he was nervous. Baksi walked straight from his corner and swung his left at Woodcock's head. Woodcock attempted two rather hesitant lefts that were short and then Joe moved in, aiming a left hook at the Doncastrian's jaw. It was an obvious punch, and Woodcock should have blocked it easily. Instead, he took fifteen stone of murderous punching-power, smack on the chin.

Bruce went down with a bang and, when he rose just in time to beat the count, a right smash to the heart and another terrific left to the head soon had him on the canvas again for 'eight'. How he managed to rise in time is a mystery, but he did so and, incredibly, stayed up until near the end of the round when he was dropped flat on his face by a blow which would have felled an ox. He had taken a fearful beating and it was a wonder of courage and endurance that he was able to continue at all.

With the clang of the gong, manager Tom Hurst sprang into the ring and, with an amazing display of sheer strength, lifted the recumbent heavyweight from the floor and carried him to his corner.

A still-dazed Woodcock answered the bell for the second, whereupon the American again began to punish him unmercifully, and people started to shout to referee Moss Dayong to stop the slaughter. What followed was a veritable shambles. Soon Woodcock's face was bruised and torn, cuts near both his eyes were bleeding freely and smearing his swollen cheeks as though they had been daubed with a crimson paint-brush. Yet, still, peering now through only one eye--the other looked like a squashed tomato--Woodcock bravely battled on and, on three occasions, he actually checked Baksi's onslaught with right hands to the body.

But it was only a momentary check and the vicious, merciless pounding went on. When the bell ended the fourth, Mr. Deyong walked across to Woodcock's corner and, as he has since recorded, asked his chief second if he did not consider that his man had taken enough.

Yet, in that fourth round, Bruce had caught Baksi with another right to the chin that had quite definitely shaken the American. If only half of the real, unpunished Woodcock had been behind that punch, I am certain that Joe must have gone down--and, most probably, stayed down.

I thought that Baksi was beginning to weaken in the fifth. Yet he never stopped hammering away with his trip-hammer blows and, by the seventh, poor Bruce's face was a ghastly sight. His mouth was a crimson slit, while there was not a sign of white skin visible under the river of his own blood. One minute and twenty seconds after the beginning of the round the referee halted proceedings.

He led the disfigured British champion back to his corner, with Woodcock stumbling along with the tottering helplessness of a little child taking its first steps. From the waist up, the gallant Northcountryman was bowed with all the pathos of extreme old age.

It was a tragic moment both for Woodcock and for Britain yet, in complete defeat, somehow Bruce remained splendid. It came as a relief, I am sure, to everyone in that packed stadium when Mr. Deyong refused to allow our Yorkshireman to fight on and it transpired later that Woodcock's jaw had been broken in the opening round. Indeed, as a result of this contest he was for a time partially blind. It was eighteen months before he fought again.

Today we all know of Woodcock's broken-jaw injury arising from that fatal first punch, and so perhaps are tempted to ask why the fight was not ended in the first round. Well, of course, the answer is that the referee had no possible way of knowing at the time that Bruce's jaw had been unhinged. Had he known, I have no doubt that he would have called a halt to the proceedings there and then.

Moss Deyong, now deceased, was one of the best and most famous referees of all time. Some years after the Baksi--Woodcock brawl he came out with a quote to this effect: '.....in that contest I was more than a referee. I was a butcher's scales, weighing bleeding beef as it was flayed for reckoning, second by second and minute by minute. It was British beef, chopped and hacked and cut for British customers by an American slaughterman....'

Arising from that one might well query his reasons for allowing the 'slaughter' to continue into the seventh round. But

let me give my own view on this point, for I feel sure that Mr. Deyong, for whose judgement I always had the utmost respect, must have seen things the same way.

In the fourth round the American had undoubtedly put everything he had into an all-out attempt to finish off his man once and for all. And he had failed. I believe that, when Deyong went across to the British champion's corner to ask if he wished to retire, Bruce's manager, Tom Hurst, himself one of the shrewdest judges in the game, must have sensed that the Pennsylvanian was about to shoot his bolt.

And, in my opinion, from the start of the fifth he no longer had sufficient strength left to apply a clean KO. I have no way of supporting this, except by going on what I might have done myself had I been in 'Mossy's' shoes, but I deduce that he decided that Woodcock had already survived so much that he was entitled, in that vital contest, to any opportunity that might remain of reversing the situation.

There will be hot controversy over the encounter for all time. The referee will, I suppose, always be the subject of criticism in certain quarters--but then that is the lot of every referee. I only know that I stand by my own judgement on the subject of boxing and boxers and I am glad to have the chance of recording yet another considered opinion on this fight. I expect this to provoke at least some laughter and rude comment, but, for all that, I think that had Woodcock not been so completely

dazed and hurt in that first round, he would have had a good chance of out-staying, outboxing and even of outpunching Baksi--in other words, of emerging the winner. As far as I know, I am the only person who has ventured to put that on paper!

When I was boxing as an amateur, I appeared on the same bill as Woodcock on several occasions round the north. Consequently, I got to know him quite well and, when I met him in later years, he was not at all averse to discussing the Baksi fight. Referring to that first left hook, which the critics called a 'sucker' punch, Bruce said that he saw Baksi standing in front of him, making a few loose probing swings with his left hand. He says that the American looked to him in no way positioned to put any real power behind a left swing, and he thought that Joe must be setting himself to throw a big right. Therefore Bruce feinted a straight left in order to test his opponent's reaction--and it was then that the pile-driving left hook came over.

To me the effect of that first blow on Bruce Woodcock's jaw makes it a 'mystery punch' rather than a 'sucker punch'. Why? I'll tell you. When Baksi clashed with Freddie Mills the previous November, he dwarfed the Britisher who was barely able to reach the huge American with his best blows. In the course of six rounds, however, Mills was never once off his feet and, what is more, was never once dazed or even staggered. I know that for a fact, and when I visited Freddie in his dressing-room almost immediately after that fight, I distinctly remember

father and I that he had never been seriously hurt by any punch. He was still quite fresh--and he did a little jig to prove it. It was purely on account of eye injuries, together with being hopelessly outreached, that caused Mills to quit for the first and only time in his career.

That night, Baksi hit Mills with everything but the ring posts and, what is more, he continued to do so for six whole rounds. How come, then, that within six months Baksi suddenly managed to develop such phenomenal punching-power?

Woodcock attended hospital for an X-Ray the following day. The doctor who examined the negative told Tom Hurst that he had only come across two other persons in the whole of his experience who had suffered dents to their temporal bones as severe as had the Doncaster boxer. The doctor added that one of these had been accidentally struck on the backswing by a man wielding a sledge-hammer, while the other had been hit by the tail-end of a backing truck. As far as I am concerned, that blow remains an alleged unsolved mystery of the ring though Woodcock has reported in print that he now knows the solution.

But, though he was not prepared to put his solution in print, I believe I know it. A hardening sedimentary solution on the bandages, undetectable at first, but eventually hardening into an overlay something like cement.

As I said earlier on, it was nearly eighteen months before the British champion was able to return to the ring and then, slowly but with tremendous determination, Bruce won one of life's greatest battles and succeeded in conquering his own fears. First, in September 1948, he knocked out 'playboy' Lee Oma, then in December he gained an unsatisfactory fourth-round disqualification verdict over Lee Savold.

At the end of March 1949 he KO'd the South African, Johnny Ralph, in three rounds at Johannesburg's Wembley Stadium. This was in the nature of a warm-up, preparatory to defending all three of his titles against Freddie Mills on 2 June on Jack Solomon's annual eve-of-the-Derby show at White City. There he put up a magnificent show, knocking out the Bournemouth hero in the fourteenth round.

Retired Joe Louis had relinquished the world title at the end of the previous year, so Jack Solomons billed the Woodcock-Mills clash as a final eliminator for the vacant crown, and he proceeded to match Bruce, as the winner, in a return against Lee Savold 'for the Heavyweight Championship of the World'. Of course, scarcely anyone believed him, but jolly Jack didn't let a little thing like that worry him!

As all the world now knows, Woodcock returned after the fourth round with a badly cut eye, when there was little to choose between the pair. It was a full-blooded right over the left eye that did the damage, and the gash it made was one of the worst I have seen. That punch confirmed for me, sitting as I was in the very front row at ringside, a theory I had, and still have, about the way in which Americans deliver their blows. This one landed with the knuckle-part of the glove, but the fist was not immediately withdrawn back to the on-guard position. Instead, after landing on Woodcock's brow, it seemed to drag outwards as the American moved to his right in a half-sidestep.

I think this may have had a lot to do with the severity of Woodcock's injury, but, digressing for a moment, it in no way explains the cut eyes which are so prevalent in British rings today. I believe these to be caused chiefly through lack of skill of the contestants, who often come charging forward head down, in pure frustration on account of their inability to make proper openings.

Returning to Woodcock and Savold. The American's claim to the world championship got no real recognition and, when he was knocked out by Joe Louis who was then attempting a comeback, the myth that the Woodcock-Savold bout was a genuine world title affair was finally exploded.

Bruce Woodcock did not retire after that defeat. On I4 November 1950, he lost his British and Empire titles to the ex-Guardsman, Jack Gardner, at Earls Court, and again an eye injury brought about his retirement, this time at the end of the eleventh round.

I feel confident that Woodcock was never the same again, either in mind or body, after losing to Baksi. I say that because it seems to me that the human frame must take years to fully

recover from the tremendous shocks of such a gruelling encounter.

The north country lad always put up a fine show, in defeat as well as in victory, but nothing will ever eradicate from my mind his wonderful display of courage against Joe Baksi in 1947. I think, now that his tale is ended, he should be judged on that one performance. And, on that, he certainly cannot be found wanting.

CHAPTER TEN: THE THIRD GREAT FIGHT BETWEEN TONY ZALE AND ROCKY GRAZIANO; FOR THE MIDDLEWEIGHT CHAMPIONSHIP OF THE WORLD, IN NEWARK, NEW JERSEY, ON 10 JUNE, 1948.

No matter how much fight-fans may appreciate a skilful battle between a pair of scientific boxers, it is the tearaway fighters and big punchers who provide the most thrills. Rough and tough brawls are uncommon in bouts involving major championships, but they are inevitable when men like Tony Zale and Rocky Graziano cross gloves.

In all three of their fights for the Middleweight Championship of the World--one of the most colourful series of all time--these natural scrappers threw away the book and fought like wildcats. So furious were the exchanges, that it was out of the question for any of their set-tos to last many rounds, yet while they did last they provided the most terrific battles seen in American rings since Jack Dempsey and Luis 'Angel' Firpo collided in 1923.

Zale's real name was Antony Florian Zaleski and his parents were settlers in Indiana who had raised five boys and two girls to go to work in the neighbouring steel mills. Tony was the youngest but one, a strong youth who spent his leisure hours in the local YMCA gymnasium. Here he first donned boxing gloves, and was soon regarded as an outstanding amateur.

He reached the final of the Golden Gloves competition in 1934, only to drop the middleweight title on a split-decision, after flooring his rival for a long count early in the bout. When he reached home, he announced to Ma and Pa Zaleski that he intended turning professional, and to direct his flailing fists towards earning cash rewards. Yet, after some two years of hard fighting, Tony returned to the steelworks discouraged--for he seemed to be getting nowhere fast in the fight-game, and win or lose he seldom left the ring without having absorbed much punishment in his efforts to get home with his haymakers.

But fighting was in his blood, and it was not long before he was pursuaded to join the stable of two notable Chicago managers, who developed his hitting and taught him how to place his punches. For the next three years he made steady progress, finally being matched over ten rounds with Al Hostak in Chicago. Now this Hostak was a vicious punching Czech from Seattle, and was recognised by the National Boxing Association of America as being world champion.

For the first two rounds he made mincemeat of Zale, flooring him twice in the process, but Tony must have absorbed some of the steel from the mills into his system, for, as Hostak tired through his own efforts, Zale came back into the picture and at the final bell was named the winner.

Naturally there had to be a return, with the title at stake, and it took place in July 1940 in Hostak's home-town. The thirteenth round saw Al huddled on the canvas, but Zale was not universally recognised as champion until more than a year later. In the meantime he defended his version of the crown on two occasions, knocking out Steve Mamakos in fourteen rounds and Hostak in two.

Then came an offer from New York to meet Georgie Abrams in a clearing-up bout, and Tony turned the trick to be universally acclaimed as title-holder with a points win at the end of November 1941. A few months after America entered the war he joined the Navy. His world title was frozen, and he did not pull on gloves again until his discharge at the end of 1945. It was hard luck, because he had been at the game for almost ten years, and he was twenty-seven.

A civilian again, he found that he was almost forgotten. His title had brought him in no cash whatsoever, but now he found himself called on to oppose a New York ringster named Rocky Graziano, who had built up a sensational record of KO victories through the medium of a dynamic right-hand.

The ring has provided a succession of colourful personalities, but no one quite like Graziano, whose real name was Thomas Rocco Barbella. He was born in a draughty New York tenement flat on New Years Day, 1922, the fifth child of impoverished Italian parents, but only the second to live longer than a few months.

Rocky learned to steal food at about the same time as he learned to walk. While still at school, he teamed up with another lad and they systematically robbed passing lorries, scrambling on the moving vehicles, and throwing off crates of merchandise. He graduated through every category of reform school, and then someone persuaded him to join a boys' club and took him in to the boxing section, where, perhaps, there might be another youth capable of standing up to this tearaway youngster and giving him a taste of his own medicine.

The result was that Rocky became a devotee of glove-fighting and before long he was cock of the amateurs. His fame as a deadly puncher spread, but, after he turned professional, several managers took him into their stables only to drop him again because he was so wild and just refused to listen to any sage advice. There was one fight-pilot, however, who liked the uncouth kid and set about the hard task of saving him from himself. This handler's name was Irving Cohen.

He kept the boy out of trouble until the Army claimed his services--an embargo which Rocky just couldn't believe, for he had scarcely realised that there was a war on! Before authority could try taming him, Graziano ran away. He was caught and sentenced to a year in prison for desertion and striking a superior officer and, after being dishonourably discharged in

1942, he returned to Cohen who was the only person alive who really understood him.

In 1943 he engaged in eighteen contests, ten of which he won by the knockout route, and the following year he had twenty bouts and chalked up another ten KO victories. Only when he came up against a man who could use the ring, dodge his power-packed rights and stab him in the face with a straight left did he drop a verdict. One man who beat him in this manner twice was crafty Harold Green. Though in each contest he was put on the canvas, Harold rose in time and managed to last out until the final bell when he gained the verdict on points.

Whether he won or lost, the fans flocked to see Rocky's special brand of ring savagery. And they howled with delight as they watched him pound opponent after opponent into the resin. He packed the huge Madison Square Garden on no less than five ocasions during 1945, winning every time by a colourful knockout. Three of those victims were 'wild man' Al 'Bummy' Davis who succcumbed in four; world welterwight champion Freddie 'Red' Cochrane who bit the dust in the tenth; and the aforementioned Harold Green who was laid out cold in three. And now Graziano was the leading contender for Zale's title.

Rocky Graziano was second only to Joe Louis as a drawing-card in American boxing at the beginning of 1946. And he enhanced his reputation with a two-round win over Marty Servo, who had just deprived Cochrane of the welterweight title,

but who never got over the effects of the beating he took from Graziano and retired from the ring without defending his newly-won laurels.

Public opinion demanded that Zale should put his title on the line against Rocky and the champion, after getting himself back into top shape via a series of warming-up outings, agreed to give 'The Rock' his chance on 27 September. The fight was staged at the Yankee Stadium, one of the great baseball parks, and some 40,000 patrons paid over $85,000 to witness one of the most thrilling slugging matches in memory.

There was no science and no ringcraft. They stood toe-to-toe and slammed, while the huge crowd roared its encouragement. The champion was made of steel, but that didn't prevent Rocky from downing him in the second round.

Still, Zale refused to stay down and he came back to catch his challenger with some terrific smashes to the short ribs. But, by the sixth round, Rocky looked ready to make his kill. And then came sensation!

A left hook exploded on Graziano's jaw, and he was floored for the full count for the first time in his life.

The fight was over, but the challenger was unaware of the fact and, when he was helped to his feet, he suddenly lunged at Zale in an attempt to continue the battle, only to be forcibly restrained by the referee and his trainer. Tony had snatched

victory from almost certain defeat with just about the last shot left in his locker--a fitting ending to a truly savage brawl.

Of course, there had to be a return contest as no one was satisfied that Zale was the master, in spite of his dramatic victory. Yet before it could take place Rocky found himself in trouble again. The Boxing Commission accused him of failing to report a bribe and Graziano, completely innocent of the charge, made a hash of his defence. So they took away his licence to box in New York State, and most of the other Commissions followed suit.

Fortunately, a Chicago promoter offered him a second chance of annexing the world title, and his suspension in Illinois was specially lifted for the occasion. When they battled the return in July 1947, defence was once again flung to the winds. The champion gave his impetuous rival such a hammering that, after the fifth round, the referee said he could allow 'The Rock' just one more session in which to try to turn the tide. He thought Graziano was in danger of losing his very life!

Rocky, half-blinded, fought on in a mist of blood and pain and with one eye completely closed. This time, however, the ending was reversed, for Graziano did precisely what Zale had done in New York and put all his remaining strength behind one right-hander that found the target.

Zale went staggering across the ring under the impact and his rival belaboured him with lefts and rights until he

collapsed into the ropes with Graziano still striking him unmercifully. The referee had to haul Rocky away and stop the contest. So the new champion had exactly evened the score by his performance in that terrific sixth round!

He tells in his book how, as he drove home to a hero's welcome, he turned to his wife and pointing to the sky said: 'As I always say Norma, somebody up there likes me'. Those last five words have since been used as the title of his autobiography.

The new champion's reign was destined to be brief--less than a year--and his short tenure of the middleweight title was anything but a happy one. A newspaper man spread the story that Rocky was an ex-convict and that he had been dishonourably discharged from the Army, so most States deprived him of his boxer's licence once again.

Luckily, Irving Cohen came up with a brainwave and he offered Rocky's services for a tournament in aid of polio victims in Washington. The champion's purse to be--just one dollar.

Consequently, Graziano went back into the ring after nine months inactivity against Sonny Horne, who had been one of his victims on the road to the top. Everybody expected the usual fireworks display, but the champ was ring rusty. He put up an exciting enough show to gain the decision, but Horne was still on his feet at the end.

The champion's action in claiming only a token purse from the charity paved the way for the lifting of his suspension in

other states. Immediately came a New Jersey offer for him to meet Zale in a decider in the Ruppert Stadium at Newark on 10 June 1948. As the contract named his purse as being 120,000 dollars, the Graziano camp leapt at the chance of risking their man's laurels for the huge sum which would be forthcoming, win, lose or draw.

For once the New Yorker trained hard, but perhaps Tony Zale trained even harder. Or maybe it was that Tony had come up the fight-ladder the hard way, whereas Graziano had reached the heights in far quicker time and therefore lacked the experience of the other. On the other hand, Zale was now past his thirty-fifth birthday, thus giving his challenger eight years.

The fact is that the receipt of severe punishment in glove fights affects some fighters more than others. There can be no doubt that both Zale and Graziano got just that in their two previous meetings and, while no man is impervious to a real belting, it would appear that Rocky could not absorb his lacings as well as did the man from the Indiana steel mills. At least, their effect disclosed itself on Rocky before it showed on Tony.

The start of the first round saw Zale jabbing with his left, while Rocky began throwing looping blows, most of which missed. Tony--remember that this time he was the challenger--got to close quarters and hammered away to the body, and Rocky lowered his arms to protect his abdomen.

Quick as a flash, Zale whipped over two left hooks that landed smack on Rocky's jaw and dropped him to the canvas. He rose at 'three', fighting mad, and tore after Tony, flailing away non-stop with both hands. Zale backed away momentarily, but then, seeming to sense that against such a rival as Graziano attack was the only real means of defence, he came back two-fisted to the body. It was now Rocky's turn to run to holds, but, on the break, he caught Zale to the head with a two-handed combination.

This only served to rouse Zale, and the pair stood toe-to-toe pounding away for all they were worth. Rocky was in his element now, and he grimaced in disgust as the bell ended the round.

In the second Zale beat his man to the punch with lefts and hooked solidly to the head, but Graziano came back with a left under the heart that had the challenger gasping and seeking a breather. Now they were both concentrating on the body, but suddenly Tony switched his blows upstairs, came inside two wild Graziano swings, and crashed in a left under the eye.

Rocky immediately got home with a left hook that made Zale blink and, though the New Yorker had to take a right in reply, he brushed it aside and tore in to the attack seemingly under the impression that he had his man going. He was raining terrific blows from either hand on Tony, but the ex-steel worker merely hunched his powerful shoulders and crossed his thick

arms so as to protect both face and body. He looked quite unperturbed as he returned to his corner at the bell.

The third was to prove the final round, but it saw Graziano leave his corner like a maddened bull, and there was scarcely a fan in the place who was not on his feet, screaming for the kill. Rocky got home with a full-blooded right, but all at once it could be seen that his blows had lost their former power. Further, he was distinctly slow to spot Zale start up his counters, and was not nearly as mobile as before. The writing was on the wall.

A Zale left and right caught Rocky as he moved ever forward, dropping him heavily, only for him to stagger gamely to his feet at 'six'. Tony Zale knew now that all danger was past and that one good blow would do the trick. So he set himself carefully before unleashing a short left hook on the side of the tottering Rocky's unprotected jaw. And that was that--Rocky Graziano was down and out, just another ex-champion.

But the colossal purse from that fight made Rocky rich. More important, however, was the fact that the fight-game had caused him to leave his old life behind. He continued to box for another four years, until Sugar Ray Robinson put an end to his ideas of making a successful comeback by whipping him in three rounds.

Then, thanks to actress Martha Raye, he became a televison star. She wanted a stooge for her show, and Rocky was

the ideal type for the job. He fitted into this comic role as if it had been made specially for him--a striking contrast to the savage ring 'killer' who had thrilled the fans with his explosive punching and won his way to the top by sheer strength and fury.

Tony Zale, I am afraid, fistically never got over those three ring duels with Graziano. He was deprived of the title little more than three months after their final meeting by the ill-fated Frenchman, the late great Marcel Cerdan, who licked him in twelve rounds.

True, he had suffered bad damage to his eyes, nose and hands in those bouts, but in boxing, the lasting damage does not always reveal itself until later--much later.

CHAPTER ELEVEN: DAVE SANDS V. DICK TURPIN; FOR THE MIDDLEWEIGHT CHAMPIONSHIP OF THE BRITISH EMPIRE, AT HARRINGAY ARENA, ON 6 SEPTEMBER, 1949.

Australia has not produced many fighters stamped in real world class, but when middleweight Dave Sands came on the scene he was looked on as the logical successor to Les Darcy, who is to this day regarded in the Antipodes as having been the greatest middleweight that ever drew breath. An aborigine, Dave came from a large and impoverished family, who lived in the backwoods of the northernmost part of New South Wales.

When the eldest boy, Ritchie, slipped away from home no one minded very much, for it was one less mouth to feed and one less lusty lad to house. In any case, he was quite capable ot taking care of himself. And when he returned several weeks later with his pockets full of money and announced that he had been boxing professionally, his parents admired his enterprise, while his brothers regarded him as a hero. Especially young Dave who was a quiet, sensitive and shy youth who loved doing things on his own.

Shortly afterwards, when his brother was scheduled to fight in Newcastle, Dave hitch-hiked his way the three hundred miles south in order that he might watch the pride of the family

perform. His brother had adopted the ringname Ritchie Sands, and did so well that he decided to remain in Newcastle, where he placed himself in the hands of a trainer and manager named Tom Maguire.

When he discovered that young Dave was there too, Ritchie suggested that he also should place himself under Maguire's banner. Tom had a gymnasium in the town and he kept and fed both the lads, as indeed he had done many boys who were homeless. But whereas Ritchie was earning his keep by fighting, his kid brother began by keeping the training quarters clean and tidy as his contribution to the bargain.

Yet, within a short space of time, Dave proved he had real ability in his fists and, on his professional debut, he proved a sensation when disposing of his rival in less than a minute. He won his first title--the New South Wales championship--by knocking out Max Cameron in eleven rounds at Newcastle in October 1945.

The following May he became Australian middleweight champion through laying low the holder, Jack Kirkham of Victoria, in twelve rounds at Sydney. Being short of rivals in his own weight division, in his very next fight he stopped another Victorian, Jack Johnson, in four rounds to add the national lightheavyweight title. Now that bout had been advertised as involving the twelve-stone-seven championship only, but, as

Johnson was also the Australian heavyweight kingpin, Sands naturally claimed both diadems as a result of his decisive win.

Johnson didn't approve of this at all, so after successfully defending the middleweight title by knocking out Kirkham in the fifth round of a return, Dave met him again in October 1946 with both the lightheavy and heavyweight crowns officially at stake. And this time he stowed Jack away inside one round, which meant that the phenomenal Sands had annexed three national championships in a total of less than seventeen rounds of fighting! Before the end of the year, Dave added the scalp of Alf Gallagher to his ever-growing list, knocking the New South Wales man out in the second round of a defence of his two heavier titles.

In 1947, Sydney Stadium Promotions imported four American fighters to meet the dynamic Sands in the persons of O'Neill Bell, Emery Jackson, Art Lind and George Henry. They all went back to the United States as losers.

Dave continued his winning run in 1948, chalking up nine more victories and thus gaining international recognition as being a 'good'un'. On the afternoon of 12 June that year the Australian got married, but he fought at Newcastle the same evening, defeating a much bigger opponent in Billy Myers, who was outpointed over twelve hard rounds.

There were two sides to Sands' nature. Sometimes this most unassuming of all Australians would fight like a demon,

throwing venomous left hooks and jabbing with perfect precision and balance before unleashing deadly right crosses, all in a matter of seconds.

But for some totally inexplicable reason--and possibly even in the same round--he might suddenly start boxing like a disinterested novice, lethargic and listless.

At the beginning of 1949, Dave and Tom Maguire visited England at the invitation of Jack Solomons. Instead of the snarling tiger of a man we had been expecting, in keeping with his ferocious punching, we met a youth with a golden-brown skin and the sensitive face of an artist who was clearly pining for his homeland. The promoter was of the opinion that, outside of champion Dick Turpin, there was no middleweight in the country good enough to stand up to Sands, so he brought over an experienced American, named Tommy Yarosz, to test the Australian. But Dave appeared to be over-awed by the Harringay big-fight atmosphere and was comfortably outpointed by his stylish rival.

On his next show, Solomons gave Sands a chance to find his true form by putting him against a Continental, called Lucien Caboche, over ten rounds. Though the Australian won beyond dispute, he was far from impressive, and on the morrow the fighter and his manager packed their bags and set off for Newcastle--the one up north, not 'Down-Under'.

Old Tom had a hunch that, if he could get Sands away from the bright lights of London, the boxer would find his feet. What better place than Newcastle, which was itself a famous fight town but on a smaller scale?

After all, it had been in the town of the same name in New South Wales where Dave had begun scrapping and where he had scored the majority of his victories. Sure enough, at Newcastle-upon-Tyne he re-established himself with two sensational and speedy wins, so perhaps the association of ideas assisted him in displaying his true form.

I was introduced to the Australians on their return to the capital, and I say without any hesitation that Dave was the most shy boxer I have ever met. During the hour or more I passed with him and his handler, he could have opened his mouth on no more than three occasions, and then only 'yes', 'no' or 'ha-ha'. Yet I watched him closely, and formed the opinion that deep down he was a charming lad, reserved and diffident, yet extremely honest and loyal.

And now Londonders saw the real Dave Sands, A brilliant win over Frenchman Robert Villemain (floored for the first time in his life) earned him a match with Dick Turpin for the latter's Empire title, the venue being Harringay and the date 6 September 1949.

Dick, like his younger brother Randolph, of whom I shall be writing later, hailed from Leamington and it was fitting that his

rise to the fistic heights had coincided with the abolition of the iniquitous 'colour bar' in British boxing. For Turpin, both from a moral and an athletic point of view, was well fitted to be the first accepted coloured boxer to win a British championship and to wear a Lonsdale Belt. He had done this by taking the British title away from Vince Hawkins in Birmingham at the end of June 1948.

The Press should be given much credit for the part its members played in obtaining justice for such British-born fighters, for many newspapers and magazines constantly attacked the British Boxing Board of Control for its colour-conscious attitude, so that eventually, though with a lamentable lack of grace, the ban was rescinded.

A word on the history of this deplorable custom. It almost certainly arose here on account of the behaviour of the then world's heavyweight champion, Jack Johnson. 'Lil Artha', as Johnson was nicknamed, refused to return to this country after depriving Tommy Burns of the championship in Australia at the end of 1908, and so violated his agreement with the National Sporting Club to put his newly-won laurels at stake against Sam Langford under their auspices.

As it was only the financial backing of that august body which had enabled the giant Negro to make the long journey 'Down-Under', his behaviour was particularly incensing. And as the sport in those days was literally ruled by the Club, perhaps it is not so strange that, when control passed into the hands of the

Boxing Board in 1929, the Club's poor view of coloured fighters was transferred with it.

Yet, that colour differentiation could still exist in this country during the twentieth century is almost unbelievable. It did, though, and while being a white was not deemed a necessary qualification for eligibility to compete for a championship in any other sport here, the Board ruled that British professional boxing championships were open only to white fighters. And this in spite of the facts that their opposite numbers, the Amateur Boxing Association, refused to draw any such line, and that the majority of the professional world champions of the time were Negroes.

I think I am the first to record that Dick Turpin's father had served with the British Army in the first World War, and that he died because his health had been undermined as the result of a gas attack on the Somme. Dick had himself served for two years with the Eighth Army in the Western Desert and he and his two brothers were the sole support of their widowed mother, who was practically blind.

After years of pugilistic campaigning, during which time he had fought and beaten practically every middleweight of note in Europe, Dick just had to be considered for a title shot as soon as the 'colour bar' was lifted. In February '48 he outscored Croydon's Mark Hart in a final eliminator at Nottingham's Ice

Rink, but before he clashed with Hawkins he was paired with New Zealand's Bos Murphy for the latter's Empire title.

Now Dick was renowned for his impeccable boxing rather than for his punching, and in his entire career he had scored no more than a handful of KO wins. Imagine the surprise of the Coventry crowd, therefore, when instead of making his usual lethargic start, Turpin knocked out the New Zealander in the opening round after first having him twice on the canvas!

Since adding the British title, the Leamington man had won a number of non-title bouts and, eleven weeks before meeting Sands, he had successfully defended both his titles against Croydon's Albert Finch.

Opinions were sharply divided as to the likely outcome of Turpin v. Sands, but my own view was that if Dick could get through the first six rounds without being nailed by one of the Australian's haymakers, he would go on to win comfortably on points. And, to tell the truth, I thought that Turpin's ring knowhow would prove too difficult a problem for Dave to solve while Dick was still fresh. Just how wrong can you get...!

It was all over in two minutes 55 seconds, and the final scene was of Turpin staggering dazedly to his feet just as the count of 'out' was called. But let there be no misunderstanding about that, for even had the referee decided that the coloured warrior had risen in time, I am sure that he would have ruled him in no fit condition to continue. For Dick had twice been down for

'nine' and had taken such a terrific hiding that just one more blow might easily have left its mark on his future health. He lost the Empire title as he won it--sensationally!

There was no hint of the drama to come as the pair left their corners at the bell. Turpin was the first to lead, but his left went over the Australian's dark head and they came to close quarters. Here Dave found that the coloured man was too clever for him, and he was unable to gain the inside berth with either of his arms, from which position he would have been able to punch away effectively.

Turpin, notoriously a slow starter, seemed content to let Sands make the running and, on the break, he moved backwards round the ring throwing out a series of long, stabbing left hands as he went. The challenger chased him to the ropes, only to be left flat-footed and off-balance by Turpin's clever side-step, the culmination of which was a quick flurry of not very powerful blows to Dave's head.

Roused, Sands moved forward again, at the same time throwing a long right. Dick saw it coming and moved inside it, but, at the very moment he did so, the Australian hooked a short left which landed plumb on the side of Turpin's jaw. It looked a dynamic-enough punch in any event, but, to make it even more devastating, extra potency was added by the fact that Turpin moved right on to it.

The Leamington man fell forward on to Sands who, stepping back, had plenty of time in which to land two further blows before the Empire champion hit the canvas. Dick was up at 'nine', but the affair was now just a procession, with Sands riding in the Lord Mayor's coach.

Instinctively, Turpin sought a respite by attempting to clinch, but this was useless for Sands uppercut him with consummate ease and then pushed him away as if he were a child.

With legs turned to jelly, Turpin lurched backwards as Dave pounced again. I think he would have gone down a second time without receiving another blow, but, as he hurtled into the ropes, the Australian got in a glancing swing before the midlander crumpled to the boards.

Only the red badge of courage enabled Dick to rise in time, and he was punched half-way round the ring before a final right dropped him in a heap again.

So dazed was he that at 'seven' he looked towards the wrong corner, seeking his seconds' advice before squirming on to one knee. At 'nine' he made a despairing effort to haul himself to his feet, but when 'out' was called he was still in the act of rising.

Sands was the new Empire champion, but as that title alone was involved Turpin remained British kingpin. Even so, he failed to get the one more notch on the Lonsdale Belt that would

have made it his own property, for, in April 1950, Albert Finch gained what I still consider to have been a very 'dodgy' verdict and so deprived him of his remaining championship.

Knowing Dick, I think he realised that, at his age, he just couldn't hope to regain his laurels and recognised the signs that his lustre was beginning to wane. So he soon announced that his days as an active ringman were through, and that he would in future devote his energies towards helping brother Randolph along the knuckle-trails.

It was certainly a fine way to quit the ring; still fit, still loving the sport and with all his virility and courage still there inside him.

After becoming Empire kingpin, Sands scored a smart victory over a tough American hill-billy named Pete Mead, but instead of going forward to even greater achievements, he went home to his beloved Australia, where he was out of the ring until March '50, when he beat a future world middleweight champion in the person of Carl 'Bobo' Olson in Melbourne. He remained 'down-under' for the rest of the year, winning five further contests.

In England, meanwhile, Randolph Turpin had become British Middleweight Champion, and he was keen to meet Sands to try to avenge the defeat of Dick. Jack Solomons liked the idea, for whichever man survived such a battle would be a logical contender for 'Sugar' Ray Robinson's world title, and early in

1951 rumours were already afoot that he was hard up for worthwhile challengers.

But Sands and Maguire remained in Australia and missed their golden opportunity. When Dave did eventually arrive in London, it was to find that Randy had already been matched with Robinson. That left the 'cobber' kicking his heels and, after winning a couple of minor bouts, he set off the the United States.

If the Australian team hoped to secure a world title tilt there, they were sadly mistaken, and after licking Olson a second time and then Henry Brimm, Sands came back to London.

Solomons featured him against Yolande Pompey, which was a good match for Sands, because the Trinidad lightheavyweight was then looming up as a contender for the world championship and victory would have put Dave right back in the picture again.

For three rounds things went Sands' way as he completely outboxed his slower opponent. Pompey seemed finished by the end of the sixth, for his mouth was so badly gashed that the crowd howled for the fight to be stopped, and his manager pleaded with him to retire.

Yet he opened a cut near Dave's left eye early in the seventh, and the blood acted like a red rage to a bull on the Trinidadian. He threw bone-crushing punches with complete abandon to take Sands clean out of his stride, and the Australian was quite helpless when the referee intervened. Yet, as he was

only a middle, this setback did not seriously affect his high ranking.

Dave spent Christmas 1951 at home and after four months, when his eye wound had healed, he walloped Ron Toohey and Chub Keith, following up by KO'ing Jim Woods during the fourth round of a defence of the Australian heavyweight crown and demolishing Al Bourke in the fifth to retain the Empire and Australian middleweight titles.

Now it was August 1952 and winter-time in Australia. After this great return to form, Maguire arranged for Sands to go to a lumbering camp in order to build himself up for a possible crack at the world title.

Brothers Alfie and Russell, themselves professional boxers, accompanied him together with other relatives who all piled into a large lorry with Dave doing the driving. Taking a bend, the vehicle skidded off the road and tumbled down an embankment.

Others were hurt, but none so badly as the Empire champion who suffered multiple injuries. He was rushed to hospital, but died without regaining consciousness. He was only twenty-six.

CHAPTER TWELVE: JACK GARDNER V. JOHNNY WILLIAMS; 12 ROUND HEAVYWEIGHT CONTEST IN THE GRANBY HALLS, LEICESTER, ON 17 JULY, 1950.

Turning a terrier pup into a bull-mastiff is something of a tall order, however one tackles the job. Really, it sounds impossible, yet in a boxing sense the task is not nearly so difficult as it would appear.

When Freddie Mills was training for his fight against Lloyd Marshall back in May 1947, an old and esteemed friend of his manager, Ted Broadribb, brought a tall, lean youngster to London to spar with Mills. Nat Seller, Mills' trainer, reported to Broadribb that the twenty-yearold seemed to have a complete fistic make-up, except in the vital asset of strength.

This was Johnny Williams from Rugby who, in those days, was hovering some way under the middleweight limit in the matter of poundage and who had been boxing professionally for just over a year. In this time he had engaged in thirteen contests, winning eleven of them and drawing one.

Broadribb decided to give the boy a chance, and offered him £25 for a week's sparring with Mills. But he later told me that the first time he saw Johnny don the gloves with Freddie he much regretted having done so. Mills nearly broke the boy's ribs, so next day the manager wanted to send him home, yet he begged to be allowed to box again.

At least that was ample proof that he was a 'game un', so the doyen of British fight managers decided that this time it was he who would take a chance. But Williams scaled only eleven stone three, had an arm span of seventy-six inches, big hands and took size eleven in boots. He looked like a big, gangling puppy, though he was so quiet and reserved that no one could say he could bark. Broadribb considered there was a hope of building him up into a big dog who could bite, and it was decided that Johnny would in future box under his guidance.

Careful feeding, plenty of the right sort of exercise and a good deal of patience were to eventually produce Johnny Williams, heavyweight, but it took some twenty months to accomplish the feat. The building-up process was so gradual and so well-timed that it happened without Johnny losing the minutest fraction of his speed, yet Williams had to suffer more than his fair share of rough breaks before he reigned for fourteen months as British and Empire champion.

By the time he became a fully-fledged member of the Beef Trust Brigade, at the beginning of 1949, Johnny had won a further eighteen out of twenty-one starts. Broadribb was anxious to bring his protege to the fore in easy stages, but in the heavyweight class in Britain there is always such a dearth of talent that anyone with ability quickly boxes himself out of opposition, and in so doing finds himself very near to being the challenger for the national championship.

It has, in fact, become obvious in recent years that a man can win the title and still be in reality little more than a novice. That, of course, is no fault of the boxers themselves, but it needs to be in one's mind when allegations are made that fighters are rushed along too quickly.

In mid-1950 Johnny Williams reached that stage, and he and another bright young prospect, Jack Gardner from Market Harborough, stood out above all others as contenders for the championships held by Bruce Woodcock.

This, even though the Rugby boy had taken part in no more than nine bouts as a heavyweight, of which he had won the lot. I knew that Broadribb did not consider that his boxer was yet ready for the title stakes, and that he would have preferred him to go on gaining experience, so that, when the time came for a tilt at the crown, there would not have been a shadow of a doubt concerning his winning it. Astute Ted was really trying to stall for a time, though he had to keep Williams working for he had his living to get and a fighter can only live by fighting.

So, on the night when Woodcock met Lee Savold for the Jack Solomons-styled version of the world championship--6 June at London's White City Stadium--Williams stepped into the same ring with a big, tough American named Pat Comiskey.

At thirteen stone five, Johnny was conceding almost two-and-a-half stones to Comiskey, who towered over the Britisher like a giant. For five rounds Williams gave a really polished

exhibition of boxing, taking every round by a street. Then, in the sixth, it happened. Johny had high, prominent cheekbones and glancing blows from Comiskey cut a deep wound under the eye. Williams had to retire from a fight which he was winning with just as much certainty as night follows day.

That spelt trouble, for less than six weeks away was the final eliminator with Gardner, for the right to oppose Woodcock in a title fight. Though Johnny's eye wound had healed well, I think that he went into that fight intent on making sure that he did not get it re-opened. Thus I believe that he gave a whole lot of confidence to his opponent, and certainly the Rugby boxer did not give his normal top-speed, scientific exhibition. But I am jumping ahead.....

Gardner was born on 6 November, 1926, which made him Williams' senior by just seven weeks. A former Guardsman, he first boxed in a unit tournament during the latter part of 1947, and so successful was he in bouts that followed that, during the early months of the following year, he was several times selected to represent the Army in international matches.

I was a fellow-member of the side which took on Wales in the annual Leach Cup match. It was the first time I had seen the big Sergeant Guardsman in a real fight, and I remember being most impressed with his power and strength, though he was at that stage of his career still very crude.

Later that same year he represented England against Denmark and Sweden, captured the Army, Inter-Services and ABA titles and, though beaten in an early series, was a British representative at the Wembley Olympic Games.

It came as no surprise when the late John Simpson, a leading manager at the time, spotted Gardner's obvious talents, made him aware of the wealth to be earned in the ring by a heavyweight with colour and a punch, bought him out of the Service and launched him as a paid performer in one of Jack Solomons' heavyweight competitions in December of '48. The ex-Guardsman won it with nonchalant ease, annihilating each of his three opponents well inside the opening round.

Between that time and when he took on Williams in the eliminator, big Jack stormed into action eighteen times, finishing a loser on only two occasions. I think, however, that the important thing to note is that he had met only two men who could possibly be termed international class - Canadian Vern Escoe twice, and the crafty French-Pole Stephan Olek.

It was Escoe who had inflicted his two defeats, though the first ot these came about when the referee halted the exchanges after five rounds, owing to Gardner having sustained a bad cut near his left eye. In the return, the Canadian clearly outscored his rival, while Gardner's win over Olek came only through a narrow points decision.

On the other hand, Williams had outpointed Escoe, and had also outscored Olek by an indisputably wider margin of points. Against this, Johnny had been able to do no better than outpoint the Swede, Nisse Andersson, while Gardner had beaten the same rival on a fifth-round retirement. Jack had, in addition, licked Scotsman Ken Shaw in seven rounds, whereas Wiliams had taken eight to do the same job.

But it was Williams who was established as a firm favourite in the pre-fight betting. There were a number of perfectly sound reasons for this, and I will attempt to list a few of them. First and foremost was the fact that the Market Harborough man had had only twenty-one contests in the paid ring as against Williams' forty-four. This was expected to be a Boxer v. Fighter affair, with Williams the lightning-fast, quick-thinking craftsman outwitting rugged, but technique-lacking Gardner. We shall see how far off the beam this train of thought was, for not only did the result 'go wrong' but the whole pattern of the fight did likewise!

At the weigh-in the inches-taller former soldier tipped the beam at 13 stone 8 and 3/4 pounds in comparision to Johnny's 13 stone 6 and 3/4 pounds, but few thought that his disadvantages either in weight or in size would seriously inconvenience Broadribb's man, for he was quite used to having to punch upwards at opponents a good deal bigger than himself.

I believe the real thing which caused most of the newspaper boys to side with Willliams, though, was that they had it in the back of their minds that the Market Harborough monster lacked a fighting brain. Certainly he could not be said to have noticeably improved since quitting the amateur ranks, and his ring moves were deemed to be stereotyped. Moreover, the right hand punch which had brough him quick success in his amateur and early paid bouts had more recently been missing. Expert opinion favoured Williams as a certain winner if the bout went the scheduled twelve-round course, but if it was to be decided inside the distance, then Gardner loked the more likely of the pair to emerge triumphant.

The first round left me wondering. We had expected Johnny to dart in and out with his rapier-like left leads, never allowing Gardner to get set to throw his heavier and more methodical blows. Instead, it was Williams who was inclined to pose, and Gardner who used his 'trombone' left hand with deadly accuracy. And that was the pattern of the fight for practically the whole of the first eight rounds, during which the Market Harborough boy built up a commanding points lead. He had never used his left hand to such effect before, and he never did so again afterwards.

Early in the contest Gardner succeeded in re-opening the gash which Williams had sustained in his battle with Comiskey, and Johnny clearly became very worried. Not that he was not inflicting plenty of damage himself, for, by the time the ninth round opened, both fighters were severely marked about the face and both had bad gashes in the vicinity of each of their eyes.

An outstanding fault in Gardner's fighting repertoire was always his irritating reluctance to belt away at an opponent's body. He did this to good effect in the gymnasium, but in actual combat he always seemed to concentrate far too much on trying to nail the small target of an oppponent's bobbing head.

A sensible fellow outside the ring, Jack often thought too slowly when inside it. With all his beef, he should have been able to throw some tremendous rights to the body, heavy drives under the heart that would have automatically brought down a man's guard. Had he adopted these tactics in the early rounds of his first meeting with Williams, I believe that he would have won inside the distance. But rather was he content to do what everyone had thought was impossible for him--*i.e.* pile up the points with the left hand, while the usually so orthodox Rugby man had to adopt the (for him) foreign role of attempting to force his way to close quarters.

Williams's seconds must have told him he was behind during the interval after the eighth round, for he left his corner for the ninth clearly bent on a knockout. And Johnny hammered Gardner all round the ring, in fact he must have won that session by such a margin as to reduce a good deal of the leeway. Yet, at the end, Jack was still on his feet and Williams' bolt had been very nearly shot.

For the record, I still think there was little between them after as gruelling a heavyweight contest as two youngsters have ever fought when they answered the bell for the final round that night in Leicester. But then Dame Fortune stepped in.

Coming out of a clinch, Williams slipped and fell right on his spine, so that he must have jarred every nerve in his body. For the rest of the round he was quite unable to conjure up a worthwhile blow. And, when the decision went in Gardner's favour, he collapsed.

It resembled the difference between a victorious and a beaten Boat Race crew. You've seen the pictures of the eights battling to the finishing line at Mortlake, and then seen the beaten crew lifeless and dejected a moment later. That's how it was with Gardner and Williams. Both exhausted but Gardner, in direct contrast to his rival, buoyed up by great elation.

Johnny was ordered to spend the night in hospital and there, feeling anything but happy, he found himself in a bed next to a fellow who asked: 'Do you know how the big fight went to-night, chum?'

Ted Broadribb has placed it on record that 'chum' replied that Gardner had won, though he didn't go out of his way to reveal the fact that he himself was the victim, because he heard the other fellow say that he had backed Williams. And he left the

hospital hoping that his neighbour had not discovered his secret!

As both Gardner and Williams continued in the ring until 1956, and especially as both were destined to win title honours and to meet each other on two further occasions, it would be inappropriate to bring this chapter to its close without giving a brief resume of their late fistic feats.

As recorded in the Woodcock-Baksi story, Jack Gardner made a successful bid for Woodcock's titles four months after his win over Williams, and he went on to capture the European crown in March 1951 by outscoring Jo Weidin of Austria.

But then Jack lost clearly to the world-ranking Argentinian, Cesar Brion, and dropped his European laurels to Hein Ten Hoff in Germany by what must have been a huge margin of points in the September of '51.

In March the following year at Harringay he put his British and Empire titles at stake in a return against Williams, who had engaged in seven bouts since their previous clash, four of them against Americans. In these Johnny had looked both brilliant and awful in turn, but a comfortable December verdict over coloured Omelio Agramonte (who had twice stayed the full ten rounds with Joe Louis on the latter's comeback campaign) had put him right back into favour.

This time Johnny emerged trimphant over his old rival, but though the battle went the full championship distance of

fifteen rounds, the pattern was altogether different from their first set-to. This time it was Williams the boxer mastering and out-manoeuvring Gardner the fighter and, while the verdict in Williams' favour received by no means unanimous acclaim, on my scorecard he was a worthy winner. I never at any stage made the ex-Guardsman in front, but occasionally he would spurt to almost clear his points deficit only to drop back into arrears when he could not maintain the hot pace. This time his left-hand work never came into the picture, though his body-punching was much improved and the margin in Williams' favour at the end must have been clear rather than wide.

Gardner announced his retirement following the loss of his titles, but he returned to the ring in December 1953 and continued to box spasmodically until April '56 when he called it a day.

In May 1953, Williams took on a Don Cockell rejuvenated by having no weight worries, and he forfeited his titles on the referee's decision after a grand scrap which was always close and interesting.

Far from disheartened, Johnny went on boxing successfully if infrequently until, in June 1955, he met Gardner for the third time in a final eliminator to determine who Cockell's challenger should be. The fight took place in Nottingham and, after holding his own for three rounds, Williams went completely to pieces and was rather ingnominously knocked out in the fifth suffering, as usual, from cuts in the region of his eyes.

The Cockell-Gardner match was secured by Jack Solomons, following Don's abortive crack at world champion Marciano, but for various reasons it was continually postponed and finally fell through altogether.

When Cockell quit the fistic scene in July 1956 without making a title defence, the Board of Control decreed that none other than Williams should oppose Cardiff's Joe Erskine for the vacant British title.

The pairing was arranged for Cardiff in late August, but well though Williams fought he was outsmarted by his younger rival. Yet even then he thought that he was capable of winning back his former laurels, and it was not until the new Empire champion, Joe Bygraves of Jamaica, easily defeated him in Manchester in November of the same year that he decided to hang up his gloves for good.

Why was it that, in their heyday, neither Williams nor Gardner got within grabbing distance of the world title? I cannot do more than put forward my own answer to that poser and, for what it is worth, here it is.

Johnny Williams had the necessary ability, but lacked the temperament which could have converted him into a world beater. Jack Gardner, on the other hand, had the temperament together with a fine physique, but he lacked the ability.

CHAPTER THIRTEEN: RANDOLPH TURPIN V. RAY ROBINSON, FOR THE MIDDLEWEIGHT CHAMPIONSHIP OF THE WORLD AT THE EXHIBITON HALL, EARLS COURT, ON 10 JULY, 1951.

Almost from the introduction of boxing as opposed to bare-knuckle fighting, the Americans have, with one exception, monopolised world championship titles in the eight originally recognised weights. There have, of course, been one or two breaks when European boxers have managed to temporarily snatch a crown and hold on to it for a short spell, but that is about all. The exception has been in the flyweight division where, since the class was instituted in 1913, Britain has had twelve holders of the world championship.

Our national successes in the winning of other world's championships have been uncommonly meagre and perhaps the reason is to be found in the fact that the Americans have gradually developed a style of fighting all their own. Since the days of dear old Bob Fitzsimmons, who won the world middleweight title by knocking out 'Nonpareil' Jack Dempsey in 1891, Britishers had made several attempts to win that title back from American keeping.

Jim Sullivan made a very gallant effort against Billy Papke in London in 1911, only to be knocked out in nine rounds. Ted Moore went the distance with Harry Greb in New York in 1924. Tommy Milligan was next to try his luck against Mickey

Walker in 1927 and Len Harvey failed against Marcel Thil in 1932. As Thil was a Frenchman, the first three were the only occasions in which we had produced men worthy of challenging American superiority and each time we really thought that we stood a reasonable chance of success. Alas, our fondest hopes were destined to be dashed!

But on 10 July 1951, Sugar Ray Robinson, Middleweight Champion of the World, met British and European Champion Randolph Turpin in a title match at Earls Court, and there has seldom been a more totally unexpected result to a big boxing contest in this country than the one accomplished by Turpin on that occasion when he won convincingly on points against all the odds.

In the whole history of pugilism it is difficult to discover a character as colourful as Robinson. Hailing from Detroit, as a youth he was accustomed to grinding poverty. When still running wild around the streets, he ran into George Gainford, known as 'The Emperor' and a boxing manager, who persuaded him to come to his Harlem gymnasium and there taught him the basic principles of boxing.

Robinson was born just plain 'Smith' in May 1920, but he always had one character trait which distinguished him from the other kids on the street. It was this: if he did something, he just had to do it well and to become top-man at it. Consequently, when he first donned the gloves, and though he was terribly

skinny and undernourished, all he wanted to do was to get in the ring under the glaring arclights and fight. Because of this driving ambition of the little coloured boy, Gainford allowed him to perform in public and 'Smith', who had no ticket authorising him to box in amateur competitions, borrowed the licence and also the name of a recently retired fighter called Ray Robinson.

And the amateurs soon discovered that they had a new overnight sensation, for on his nineteenth birthday the newly-christened Robinson won the Golden Gloves title in the featherweight class. Next year he became champion in the lightweight division and soon after his twentieth birthday he made his professional debut at Madison Square Garden. That was on 6 May, and Ray scored a two-round KO victory. Win after win followed and, by the end of the year, Robinson was well known.

In 1941 he achieved national fame, and cemented this by licking ex-world welterweight king Fritzie Zivic on the last day of the year. Some two weeks later he repeated the win--this time through a tenth-round knockout--and now it was obvious to all that he was on the way to the very top of the fistic tree. Four of his victims, about this time, were boxers who had held world titles--one of them being the then reigining lightweight champion, Sammy Angott, and another former triple champion, Henry Armstrong.

There can be little doubt that the majority of boxers campaigning in the welterweight division wanted no part of Robinson, so he was forced to tackle middleweights in order to keep busy. Therefore, it was not until December 1946 that he was given a crack at the world welterweight title, and then he won it by comfortably outpointing Tommy Bell, the champion, in Madison Square Garden, just five days before Christmas.

Despite the notoriety which his flashing black fists earned him, Robinson had his troubles. He had been freely criticised in the American Press because of a rumour that he had been dishonourably discharged from the U.S. Army, but he was able to prove the rumour false and to show that he had been discharged on medical grounds.

It had also been bandied about that he was mean and slow to assist fighters of the same colour skin who were down on their luck. Though his answer to this was that he wished to invest his money wisely and so not be forced to rely upon the charity of others himself, there seems little room for doubt that Ray was not a particularly popular or likeable character until his meeting with Jimmy Doyle in 1947--a meeting which had a tragic and fatal ending and which seemed to have the effect of bringing the welterweight champion to his senses.

A title bout in Cleveland, Ohio, saw Sugar Ray stop the strong and game Doyle in eight rounds. Jimmy, who had previously been suspended following a knockout defeat, never regained consciousness after the bout and died in hospital next day. Doyle's family were far from being well-to-do, and Robinson did everything he could to help them in their distress.

This incident appears to have marked the start of Robinson's great interest in the fight against cancer which was to make him a leading figure on the board of the Damon Runyon Cancer Fund. Sugar Ray later gave away thousands of dollars to this cause.

By August 1950, Robinson was finding difficulty in making the welterweight limit of ten stone seven pounds and so he relinquished the title. In February 1951, after prolonged negotiations, he was matched with an old opponent, Jake La Motta, for the world middleweight title. La Motta had been champion since June 1949, when he had taken the crown off the head of the ill-fated Frenchman, Marcel Cerdan. And since that time he had twice successfully defended it against Italy's Tiberio Mitri and Laurent Dauthille of France. They nicknamed La Motta 'The Bronx Bull' on account of his great strength and durability, and he was the only man to have beaten Ray up to this time--he did so in 1943 though Robinson had proved the winner in an earlier meeting.

La Motta, like the game and talented fighter he undoubtedly was, gave his all in trying to retain his coveted championship. Yet he had to be rescued by the referee in the

thirteenth round of a fight that had developed into a veritable massacre.

So now Robinson was recognised by most of the world's boxing authorities as one of the outstanding fighters of the century, and one truly in the tradition of the great coloured boxers, such as Jack Johnson and Joe Gans. He was, in fact, considered to be invincible at or anywhere near his own weight.

The scene shifts to Leamington Spa, near Birmingham, where dwelt the coloured family Turpin. There were three brothers, Dick, Jackie and Randolph. Dick, as I have already mentioned, had earlier become the first coloured boxer to hold a British national professional title, an honour which he lost in 1950. Jackie was a more-than-useful featherweight, while, by March 1951, Randolph, though the baby of the family, held the British and European middleweight titles.

Born on 7 June 1928, he soon made his mark as an amateur by capturing an ABA junior championship. Then, in 1945, he won the ABA senior welterweight title and followed up next year by annexing the middleweight crown. There is no doubt that Randy owed a great deal of his success to the early coaching of his brother, Dick, and it was not surpising that, when he decided to commercialise his fists, he should join the stable of George Middleton, the man who had piloted both his brothers.

I well recall how, in September 1946, I spoke to Randy at a weigh-in in Jack Solomon's old gymnasium--that night he was to

make his debut in the professional ring at Harringay in a six-round supporting contest to the Lesnevich-Woodcock battle. He was on leave from the Navy in which he was serving as a cook, and was wearing uniform.

Several times I had boxed on the same bill as Turpin in the amateur ranks and I remember how pleased he looked when I said: 'I'm sure you'll find the first few bouts as a pro' much easier than some of those you've been having lately as an amateur. Don't forget that in those recent international matches you've been meeting and beating some of the best amateur middleweights in the world'.

That night Randy annihilated one Gordon Griffiths well inside the first round, and by the end of the year he had recorded a hat-trick of good wins. Right from the beginning of his professional career, Turpin demonstrated the tremendous punching power that had made him tops in amateur boxing. He went through 1947 without a defeat, nine of his thirteen opponents failing to stay the distance.

In September 1948, Randy met with a serious reverse when he was forced to retire after five rounds against the Frenchman, Jean Stock. Stock had, however, been on the canvas for several long counts in the early stages of the bout and it was a damaged hand which brought about Turpin's retirement. It is worth recording that, in 1951, he got full revenge over the Frenchman when he beat him in five rounds at Leicester.

Ninteeen-forty-nine saw Turpin really come into his own, winning all but one of his eight fights inside the distance. After four more wins the following year, he was matched with Albert Finch in October for the British title which Albert had annexed from brother Dick Turpin. Strangely enough, Finch had also been the first man to conquer Randy, over whom he had been awarded a points verdict back in April 1948.

The fight took place at Harringay and Randy knocked out Finch in five rounds after subjecting his man to a merciless body assault. It was not long before he added the European crown by sensationally knocking out the Dutchman, Luc Van Dam, in just over a minute of the opening round.

As world champion Robinson had taken nearly four rounds to do the trick against the Netherlander, it was natural that tremendous interest was thus aroused in a prospective world title clash between Robinson, the fabulous champion, and the dynamic-punching Britisher.

I know that manager Gainford at first demanded a guarantee of £30,000 for Robinson's services, but whether he relented somewhat under promise of a return-fight clause being inserted in the contract for use in the event of his champion being beaten in not clear. However, terms were agreed between the Americans and promoter Jack Solomons, and the pair were signed to meet at the Exhibition Hall, Earls Court, on 10 July 1951. It was a sell-out within hours of the match being announced--in fact, within a few days the promoter's staff had to return thousands of pounds to would-be-patrons.

The champion arrived in this country with a chain of handlers which soon came to be known as 'The Robinson Circus'. Sugar Ray set up his training camp at those famous old quarters, The Star and Garter, Windsor, while Turpin went to Gwyrch Castle in North Wales. Robinson, particularly, made the best fight copy that had come the way of the Press for years and they really gave him and his entourage the treatment. By the time the day of the fight arrived London was obsessed by fight-fever.

A huge crowd blocked Great Windmill Street, where the weigh-in was held at 1pm on the day of the fight, and Robinson had to be assisted by a specially-summoned police escort when he arrived in his huge Cadillac. Otherwise, he could never have forced his way into the premises which housed the scales.

Expert opinion overwhelmingly favoured Robinson to retain his title and, as far as the general public were concerned, those who sided with Turpin did so more through wishful thinking than from real confidence in his chances of bringing off an upset victory.

Everyone in London seemed to be making their way to Earls Court that night, and the ticket spivs must have made one of their best-ever profits outside the arena. I went to the fight by car and, as we crawled along the Brompton Road, I distinctly remember my companion remaking: 'I wonder how Randy's

feeling now'. And I thought: 'I wonder!'. Though he had looked very relaxed and at ease at the weigh-in earlier in the day, it is those last few hours before ringtime which stretch a fighter's nerves to breaking-point and when the mask of confidence for such a match as this is liable to fall off.

Solomons always played up the incomparable thrill of a big-fight night to the full when his top-liners entered the arena. The spot-light picked them up--first the challenger, then the champion--the excited crowd let loose a land-sliding roar and then came the fanfare of trumpets booming out with a metallic crash. On this occasion the roar of the crowd greeting Turpin almost drowned that piercing fanfare.

As soon as the boxers had entered the ring and the ring lights were once more switched on--the entry of the gladiators is made more dramatic by the dousing of all arena lights, barring the 'spot'--I became aware of an atmosphere almost superhuman about Turpin. While Robinson pranced around in his corner limbering up, Randy watched him, and when the pair shed their wraps there seemed to be something resembling a glowing, glossy sheen on the surface of the British boxer's skin. And that is a sign that a man has reached the absolute peak of physical fitness. Had the crowd not been so dense at the weigh-in, I suppose, I would have spotted it then, but, as it was, I suddenly sensed that, whatever the ultimate result might be, our man was

destined to give a very good account of himself. Yet I am sure I never dreamt of the course that the exchanges were to take.....

It was apparent as early as the first round that the champion had no defence against Turpin's exploitation of the good old English straight left. So complete was Randy's supremacy in the early rounds that it seemed that Sugar Ray was deliberately enticing him into a trap or, perhaps, boxing at half-speed for a while in order to give the patrons a real show before going into his 'killer' act. He had done this often during recent bouts on the Continent, where he had been known to deliberately 'carry' an opponent along for a few rounds. But, even so, surely even the great Ray Robinson could not enjoy being the recipient of those powerful lefts?

Then in round seven, Robinson really staggered the British boy, only for him to fight back fiercely and force the American backwards round the ring. Turpin continued to take the initiative and the champion had to box on the retreat for most of the remainder of the fifteen rounds.

As round succeeded round, the eighteen thousand people in the arena could scarcely believe what they saw, with Turpin outboxing and outfighting the champion; yet suddenly they seemed to realise that, barring an accident, the title must change hands. Robinson was badly handicapped after the half-way mark by a cut eye, which bled freely right to the final bell.

But it was Randy's sheer boxing magnificance that night which made such a fine champion as Robinson appear ineffective.

The crowd was on its feet in the last round. Men danced in the aisles, while most of the women present were either screaming with excitement or weeping with pent-up emotion.

At the final bell Eugene Henderson, without hesitation, raised Turpin's hand in token of victory and, indeed, such must have been the margin of Randy's triumph that the referee had no need to first check his scorecad.

The ring resembled bedlam, being invaded by Turpin's supporters and then, spontaneously yet gradually at first but rising to a crescendo of sound, the song 'For He's A Jolly Good Fellow' was taken up among the vast crowd. And why not? For Randolph Turpin had become the first Briton to wear the title 'Middleweight Champion of the World' since revered Bob Fitzsimmons.

Sad to relate, his reign as such was destined to be short for, honouring that 'return bout clause' in his contract, Randy met Sugar Ray again just two months later on his own 'midden', New York. Again he boxed superbly and, by the start of the tenth round, was miles ahead on points. Robinson's eye was again badly cut--this time the wound was indisputably worse than on the occasion of their first clash--on top of which the Britisher appeared by far the stronger man.

In the tenth Sugar Ray, like the great fighter he was, sensed that he might be forced to quit through his injured optic and made an all-or-nothing effort. Turpin took a 'nine' count, then took refuge on the ropes bobbing, weaving and rolling under a hail of leather, yet still managing to make the larger portion of blows land off target.

However, Ruby Goldstein, a top American referee, stepped in with only two seconds remaining of the round and declared that Robinson had regained the crown. It is likely that, had the round been completed, the bout would have been ended in Turpin's favour owing to Ray's cut eye--which, by the way, required eight stitches afterwards.

For, in America, it is a Boxing Commission doctor who decides whether a fight should be stopped in this way. And I have been told by an eye-witness who was seated behind Sugar Ray's corner that this official was waiting to climb into Robinson's corner to examine the wound at the end of that tenth round.

Nevertheless, when Randolph Turpin made Sugar Ray Robinson appear 'just another fighter' that summer night at Earls Court, he won himself undying fame as one of Britain's 'Immortals Of The Ring'.

CHAPTER FOURTEEN: JAKE TULI V. HONORE PRATESI; 10 ROUNDS FLYWEIGHT CONTEST AT THE ROYAL ALBERT HALL, LONDON, ON 4 NOVEMBER, 1952.

Number 25, Brooklands Avenue, Sidcup, Kent, was a pleasant six-roomed semi-detached house with a garden, back and front. With a car, a television set, washing-machine, vacuum cleaner and friendly neighbours there was little more that the Tuli family, who lived there until April 1958, could have wished for.

The place contrasted oddly with a tiny brick and iron building in the coloured township of Noordgesig, near Johannesburg, to which Jake Tuli, the little Zulu who reigned as Empire flyweight champion from September 1952 to October '54, returned with his wife Peggy, and their three children.

Tuli made the decision to go back to South Africa after he had been warned by doctors that he must take his younger son, John, to live in a warmer climate. Shortly after his arrival back in his native land, my friend Jake wrote me a letter in which he said: 'It was a hard decision to take, for I knew that my whole family would have to make their home in one eleven-foot by six-foot room and, in any case, my parents were dead and I loved London. When Peggy and I closed the door of number 25 for the last time we both wept a little....' This tiny gentleman of the ring closed his letter by expressing the hope that '....when John is

older and stronger, maybe we'll go back to London and meet up with you again'.

It never happened and I am sorry because the Tuli family were some of the nicest people it has ever been my good fortune to meet. A staunch church-goer, Jake was a credit both to his race and to tbe boxing game generally, and he left nothing but pleasant memories with those he met during his sojourn in England. The fact that he earned thousands of pounds through his fists while he was among us is purely incidental.

The Tuli story really begins in Noordgesig on 7 July 1931, for it was here that he first saw the light of day as John N'Tuli. Like so many good fighters-to-be, his early years were spent in conditions of extreme poverty. Like most youths, he got into his fair share of scraps at school, but was taught the rudiments of the noble art at a Roman Catholic Boys' Club and was fighting professionally before his nineteenth birthday.

Legal restrictions in South Africa then made it impossible for coloured folk to engage in sporting competitions against whites, so Jake's opportunities were much limited, his bouts were few and far between. By the end of 1951 he had boxed only six times, winning on each occasion, but his hurricane all-action style of fighting had nonetheless made him into a great drawing-card throughout the Union.

And when, after this, he added, in successive battles, the Transvaal flyweight title and the South African non-European fly

and bantamweight crowns his fame spread as far afield as London.

Portly manager, Jim Wicks, then one of the most respected in all Britain, imported Tuli here and pulled off what turned out to be a master-stroke by arranging for his debut to be made against Teddy Gardner at the St. James' Hall, Newcastle, on 8 September 1952. Now Teddy hailed from West Hartlepools, and he was the reigning British, Empire and European eight-stone champion. Promoter Joe Shepherd was anxious to have Gardner top his bill, but he was not over-keen to have what was virtually an unknown quantity occupy the opposite corner for fear that lack of a big-name opponent might have an effect on the gate.

Wily Wicks suggested that, if the match were billed as involving Gardner's Empire title, it would prove a far bigger attraction and Shepherd was not slow to see the sense of this. He put the idea to the West Hartlepools man who, apparently thinking he was on an easy thing and remembering that he was, in any case, boxing on a percentage of the gate, readily agreed. Further, as the coloured boy was only eligible to box for the Empire crown, his other titles were suitably protected, even in the event of his being defeated.

What a turn-up for the book the packed house witnessed! For what Tuli did to the bald-pated northerner was nobody's business and, after giving a whirlwind display of non-stop

aggression which reduced his rival's usually immaculate defensive skill to naught, the referee intervened in Jake's favour during the twelfth round. His win put the Zulu under the spotlight of firece publicity and, after another inside-the-distance victory at the Newcastle arena, he was booked for a big fight against France's Honore Pratesi at the Royal Albert Hall, London, on 4 November.

Two-and-a-half years previously, the Frenchman had come close to winning the world flyweight title in a set-to with Terry Allen at Harringay, while the year before Allen won the championship Honore had actually outpointed him when making a sensational London debut. That had been in 1949, the year during which he had annexed the French title by beating Louis Skena. There was quite a story about Pratesi.

He did not take up boxing until he was past his twenty-second birthday and a married man. Marseilles was his birthplace, and it was there that one day his father took him to the local gymnasium which was run by Phillippe Filippi, a well-known fight-monger. Papa Pratesi was tall and big, while Honore was extremely small and skinny and it seemed a big joke when it was suggested that the dwarf-like figure should don the gloves.

The real reason behind his father's desire for Honore to be taught to defend himself lay in the fact that his son was employed in a mental-home for violent lunatics where he was quite liable to be assaulted at any time. So under Filippi's

watchful eye, Pratesi began to train and he became a proficient boxer remarkably quickly. Speed was his forte and when he began to compete in amateur bouts, he ran up a string of thirty-six straight wins in less than two years.

When Honore suggested to his instructor that he should turn professional, the latter replied that at twenty-four Pratesi was well past the ideal age for entering the paid ranks. Almost as an afterthought, Filippi added that, as his charge performed more like a youngster of eighteen, maybe it was not too late for him to get a living out of boxing.

So the Frenchman doffed his amateur singlet once and for all, and within four years he was champion of France. Jack Solomons staged the Allen-Pratesi world title meeting, and it was certainly a contest to be remembered. The pair tore into each other incessantly for the whole fifteen rounds and there was scarcely a clinch. Apart from the necessity of having to render what must have been an extremely close verdict in the Englishman's favour, the referee had the easiest task imaginable.

The excitable French party were somewhat upset and irascible because they considered that Honore had done enough to win, but they swallowed their natural disappointment and left for home the following afternoon determined that their man would one day prove himself to be without doubt the best flyweight in the world.

As very often happens in the fight-game, this setback began a run of ill-fortune, and when Pratesi next appeared in London he was awarded only a draw against the bagpipe-playing Scot, Vic Herman. And this time I felt that he was definitely the victim of a raw deal.

Then, in his home town of Marseilles, fellow-countryman Emile Chemama put him away in seven rounds. Worse was to follow, for Skena regained the French title and although Honore secured a match with Jean Sneyers in Brussels in November '50, for the European crown, he was vanquished inside three rounds.

Only once did he go into action during the ensuing fifteen months, but made a welcome full-scale return to the ring in 1952, winning several contests and showing his very brightest form. Though he was now in his thirty-first year, he was apparently back at his best and looked a real threat to any man near his weight in the world.

So when Honore was matched with Tuli, it seemed that he was just the person to test the rising Zulu to the full, and that was the way it turned out to be in a sparkling fight. Indeed, the majority of the Albert Hall fans thought that the Frenchman had earned the decision. As for me, I still consider that the contest would have made a perfect draw.

The two tiny figures, one white, the other brown, danced round and round each other with gloves flashing, thrust and parry. This was pure boxing, and the fans loved every second of it. The more experienced Frenchman was masterly in his moves and his footwork was brilliant. On the other hand, the young Zulu obviously carried the heavier punch and was continually the aggressor.

It was entertaining stuff and the crowd applauded unstintingly at the end of each session. For the first four rounds Pratesi outboxed his rival, but then he slowed down a trifle and Tuli jabbed and hooked until the Frenchman's face was like a red mask.

By the end of the ninth stanza Jake had made up his arrears and had only to maintain the initiative to earn the decision. But, from somewhere, Pratesi unearthed fresh reserves of strength, and the two battled away at a breathtaking pace.

Honore simply swarmed over his rival and Jake had to give ground. Inch by inch he was driven back until, with his back to the ropes, the Zulu whirled both gloves unceasingly in his effort to hold off the indomitable Frenchman. If ever a man tried to snatch a fight out of the fire that man was Pratesi. He kept his gloves going at full blast and when Jake's seconds cried ' last ten' to Tuli he joined in and they finished the fracas punching it out toe-to-toe.

At the final bell they embraced and then departed to their respective corners to await the referee's decision. I totted up my scorecard, which I always kept on such occasions, and found that I made the fighters' total points equal. Some loud-mouthed

ringsider opined that 'the froggy's skated it!' while his neighbour could be heard remonstrating with him 'not to be so higgerant'.

When Tuli was named the winner, the crowd did not like it at all. As there was prolonged booing, presumably the Frenchman's wonderful last round rally had swayed them in his favour. There were tears in Pratesi's eyes as he congratulated his conqueror, and the little Zulu warrior himself led the applause in appreciation of a fine performance by a gallant loser. Honore acknowledged his reception, and there was a fresh outburst of disagreement as Tuli left the ring. It seemed no different from the climax of many another close bout.

A couple of middleweights went on next, and they commenced pounding away with not much science but heaps of enthusiasm. Midway through their set-to a rumour reached the ringside that Pratesi had collapsed and that an ambulance had been sent for.

Down in the basement of the arena there was a crowd outside the dressing-room door that had the Frenchman's name scrawled across it, and inside the partially dressed Honore was lying on the rubbing-table with a blanket drawn across his chest. His hands were tightly clasped to his forehead and his face had a deathly pallor about it.

He did not answer when the doctor spoke to him, and the medics looked extremely worried. One or two of those standing around also wore anxious expressions, and somehow there was

an air of gloom pervading the whole atmosphere of the place. The door opened and two ambulance men came in bearing a stretcher. Frankly, I was only too glad of the chance to make a surreptitious exit. And yet, somehow, I couldn't credit what I had seen, though I sensed that there was little hope for poor Honore Pratesi.

I was only on pleasure bent that night, and so did not have to return to the ringside, but, as I left the arena, I ran into a friend. He had seconded a boxer who had performed earlier in the evening and who shared Pratesi's changing quarters. My friend disclosed that, on the Frenchman's return to the dressing-room after his fight, he sang cheerily while taking a shower-bath, started to dress, but suddenly complained of feeling cold and ill. Then he collapsed.

My friend and I had a drink, and then I phoned the hospital to which Pratesi had been taken. But it was too soon for them to be able to give any information. I should have known that, but I think I hoped that having well-wishers inquire for him might in some way help the stricken boxer.

Next day two delicate brain operations were performed in an attempt to save his life, but to no avail. Pratesi died on 6 November and, at the inquest, the coroner said: 'Boxing fatalities are fortunately rare things in this country. I think this is a tribute to the way in which fights are conducted by the British Boxing Board of Control'. Well, nowadays I'm not so sure about that.......!

Little Jake Tuli was broken-hearted. At first he wanted to give up fighting altogether, but after talking it over at great length with a priest, with whom he was very friendly, he was persuaded to change his mind. However, he donated the entire purse for his next fight, in which he knocked out Emile Delplanque in four rounds at Nottingham, to Pratesi's widow.

The Frenchman's tragic end remains something of a mystery, for although it is known that injuries to the brain brought it about, he certainly was the recipient of no really severe punishment in the Tuli fight. Of course, the degree of damage to the brain cannot be assessed on the evidence of any one fight, rather must one delve into the past and, in the case of Honore Pratesi, I am at once struck by his stoppage at the hands of Jean Sneyers and his KO defeat by Emile Chemama--though, as I recorded earlier, both these reverses took place some two years previous to his clash with the Zulu. I did not see either of those affairs, and so am in no position to judge the severity of the beatings which Honore had to take. Therefore, I say that those bouts are the only ones I can find in his record as a professional boxer which might provide the key to the mystery of his having sustained lasting brain injuries.

Tuli hung on to his Empire title until October '54, when he was outpointed by Dai Dower in a classic encounter at Harringay. What a night that was, for hundreds of the Welshman's fans chartered two special trains to make the journey from Abercynon, and they invaded the capital sporting rosettes, leeks and 'Dower Will Win' posters. No sooner had Dai entered the ring--even before the Empire champion arrived--than the singing of traditional Welsh airs began. But the Zulu got a big hand, too, and the entire battle was contested in the midst of a tension so concentrated one felt it could be cut with a knife.

We all knew that if Jake could only get to close quarters for long enough to slow Dower with his powerful body-punching combinations, it would only be a matter of time before he found the Welshman's chin with the 'old equaliser'. Yet Dai boxed superbly and, though he was in difficulties on several occasions, he piled up points almost exclusively through his straight left to run out a worthy winner.

During the next twelve months fly and bantamweights alike fell before the South African's flailing fists, but in September '55 he unsuccessfully challenged bantamweight kingpin Peter Keenan for his Empire laurels--which set-to I shall describe briefly in a later chapter.

In my opinion that was the last time we saw the truly great Tuli, for when he fought a return with Dower three months later he was only a gentle breeze compared with the hurricane we once knew, and he finished dead tired and well beaten. His final bouts in British rings were as a featherweight, but I prefer to erase those 'necessity' contests from my memory because they showed gentleman Jake as a fighter with a spent battery.

I know how hard manager Wicks tried to prevent Tuli taking the pitcher to the well too often, and I also know that, when he realised the little fellow's need, he refused to deduct his percentage from the boxer's purse on those last outings. And I suspect that Jake would never have boxed as a featherweight at all had he been allowed to take up his occupaton as a qualified machine-minder in the printing trade when he first contemplated retiring from the ring. To our shame, when he sought positions in this category his colour was held against him.

Tuli had one more fight after returning to South Africa, after which he said: 'I shall never fight again'. He had just been well outpointed over ten rounds by John Mthimkhulu, having taken two long counts. Only his gameness allowed him to last the full course.

When last the Zulu wrote to me, many years ago, he enclosed a photograph of his two sons. They were seen at play in the dirt road outside their home with other coloured children. The wheel of fortune had turned full circle.

CHAPTER FIFTEEN: 1953 AND FAREWELL TO TOMMY FARR--THIS TIME FOR GOOD.

The scene was Nottingham Ice Rink: the date 9 March 1953, and the time approximately nine-forty in the evening. Tommy Farr, late of Tonypandy in Wales but more recently of Brighton, was angry--angry because the referee had just refused to allow him to continue after the seventh round of his British and Empire heavyweight title final eliminator with Don Cockell owing to a bad cut near his left eye. And, though he must have realised rounds earlier that he could not win, Tommy had so much wanted to be allowed to go down fighting.

Yet the old warrior from Tonypandy--Farr was now just three days short of his thirty-ninth birthday--stole the show at the finish, for he grabbed the microphone and began to sing from his heart the Welsh National Anthem, 'Land of My Fathers'. Looking round the 6,000 capacity stadium, it seemed to me that the place had suddenly transformed itself into one huge Welsh choir.

I'm not ashamed to admit that I had a lump in my throat that night, for I'm quite sure that the same thing applied to nearly every person in that packed hall. I looked up at the scarred face of the great old Welsh battler, and I remembered.......

That way back in 1926, at the age of twelve, he began fighting for fame and fortune, but that his talents were recognised only grudgingly after years of hard striving. For Farr had risen out of the depths of the squalor and poverty of the Welsh pits, and I was sorry that one who had fought so hard and so long before finally succeeding should have been forced into a comeback which meant spilling more blood for his wife and three children. It was in 1940 that he had first kissed the fight-game goodbye, with a nice swag in his pocket, and he had collected ten years of ring-rust when the comeback began, but more of than anon.......

No fighter can have made a more disastrous debut in London than did Farr. It took place at the old Crystal Palace in 1933 under the promotion of the late Sydney Hulls senior who, incidentally, was the father of my friend Sydney Hulls junior, sometime well-known as a Daily Express sportswriter. Hulls had matched one of Phil Scott's 'white-hopes', Eddie Steele of Norwood, with the Welsh lightheavyweight Randy Jones. But Jones was injured a few days before the fight and the promoter was advised to take as substitute the young Tonypandy miner called Farr who, a month earlier, had licked Jones.

Reports of the Farr-Steele clash show that it was a shocking fight. There was much holding and slapping and little real action. So much so that after six rounds the crowd began to slow-handclap together with rhythmic stamping of their feet. But then, in the seventh, Steele landed a moderate blow on Tommy's throat and, to the general amazement, the Welsh boy stopped boxing, vaulted the ropes and went tripping up the aisle to his dressing-room with Steele, the referee and his own seconds looking after him in astonishment.

The effect Farr's action had on his popularity can be imagined. Tommy disappeared into the Welsh hills for nearly twelve months, during which time he remained undefeated in fifteen bouts, including winning the Welsh cruiserweight title off the aforementioned Jones.

He returned to the capital in February '34 to drop a verdict to Eddie Phillips, and a year later again went under to the Bow boxer in a British cruiser title bout. Farr just could not crash into the big-time, though, from June that year, when fellow-countryman Jack Petersen annexed the heavyweight titles from Len Harvey, Tommy was always right on his tail trying to obtain a title match. But he could get recognition neither from the Board of Control nor from the country's leading promoters. They did not consider the miner from Tonypandy to be 'box-office', even though he beat two ex-world lightheavyweight champions in the persons of Tommy Loughran and Bob Olin. London fans just did not like him.

This caused him to nurse a grievance about the opposition to him, and also about what he considered to be a grave injustice in the matter of Petersen's avoidance of meeting him in the ring. However, in August '36 Ben Foord relieved Jack of the championships and, being something of an uninspired titleholder with no real international pretensions, he agreed to place them on the line against the kid from Tonypandy at Harringay Arena the following March.

Farr won on points to become British and Empire champion, but the fight itself must rank among the dullest of all big fights between heavyweights, and Tommy had still not won his way into the hearts of the London fans.

I am convinced that it was only his sincere conviction that all the world was against him which transformed Farr into the great fighter he undoubtedly became. For I saw that clash with Foord and, to be frank, when he was named the winner I was one of the many who left the north London arena thinking that we had seen just another poor champion crowned.

Now it happened that earlier Sydney Hulls had gone to the United States with the fixed intention of bringing back Max Baer to meet Jack Petersen. In the meantime, however, Jack had dropped his title to Foord who, in his turn, had also become an 'ex-champion'. So Hulls was committed by contract to give Baer a fight, and he suggested that he should oppose the German, Walter Neusel, but the Board of Control refused to permit a match between two foreigners to take place in this country. Therefore, the impresario had no alternative but to cut his losses and engage Farr.

Most Englishmen still believed that Tommy couldn't fight and that it was legalised murder to throw him in with Baer. My father was very friendly with Hulls, and he has told me that even the promoter himself was not at all happy about the pairing. Yet Farr completely outboxed and out fought Baer to upset the 'wide boys' odds of 10-1 against him, and he made the fickle boxing public completely change their attitude towards him. That night at Harringay the crowd rose to its feet as one man at the end of the fight and, though few but the loyal Welshmen among the 11,000 crowd could have known the words, hummed in tune as the day-excursion boys up from the valleys sang 'Land of My Fathers'. And why not, for had not Tommy-bach won on points by the proverbial mile?

Never had a British big man handled a top American with the ease with which Farr mastered Baer, and Max was a former World Champion and was one of the most devastating right-hand punchers of the last twenty-five years. There he was, bemused, beaten and thumbing away the blood as it continued to pour down from a cut above his left eye as he sat, tired and dejected, in his corner.

Thus, in twelve rounds of boxing, the Welshman achieved what he had failed to accomplish in years of striving--the adulation of the fans. In addition, he was now a contender for the world title.

Walter Neusel, the big blond German who had beaten Foord and emerged triumphant on no less than three occasions against Petersen, was the next importation booked to share the Harringay ring with Farr, l5 June 1937 being named as the big day. A completely confident Tommy made his rival look like a novice as he outspeeded and outfought him for two rounds. A left and a right cross flush to Neusel's chin dropped him heavily in the third. He made some kind of attempt to rise, but was counted out still on one knee. Von Ribbentrop was at the ringside, but at this he stalked out in anger!

Delighted Sydney Hulls now made a match between Farr and Max Schmeling to take place at London's White City. Contracts were signed but Mike Jacobs, promoter at Madison Square Garden, New York, badly wanted an attractive opponent for the new world kingpin, Joe Louis (who had just given heavyweight boxing a shot in the arm by depriving 'old man' James J. Braddock of the title) and he made a handsome offer to Farr to challenge Louis in New York that August.

Though he was under contract to Hulls, the Welshman accepted the Louis fight--I am sure that he feared that if he declined the offer Schmeling might step in in his stead and so deprive him of his big chance for good.

Literally no one, either here or on the other side of the water, conceded him any chance with the Brown Bomber, especially as there were whispers that the Britisher's eye had been cut in a sparring session a few days before the fight.

It was a bad start, too, when he was called to the ringside a long time before the fight was scheduled to begin. He was forced to sit watching the final rounds of a preliminary bout, which is far from the ideal way of spending the last few minutes before entering the arena for a major fight.

Yet, when the bell went, Tommy walked straight into Louis as if he were just one of his sparring-partners and he plastered the world champion's features with a honey of a left. Joe, puzzled by the Welshman's crouch and clever defence, took a long time settling down, but when at last he did so he opened up a cut beneath Farr's right eye.

The harder Louis crashed in right crosses, the more determined the Welshman became, as he kept boring-in, forever on the attack. Round seven was the highlight of the fight, when three murderous hooks sent the challenger spinning across the ring. Another thump brought blood from his other eye, but still Farr, spitting blood and thumbing it from both eyes now, kept moving forward. This was the crisis round, and it was the one which won the crowd over to the side of the Britisher.

Though he had survived heavy punishment, Tommy won the eighth and ninth. Had he possessed a real KO dig in his right he would probably have won the battle there and then but, alas,

Farr was never really a puncher though he made an awful mess of Joltin' Joe's face with his left.

Now it was Louis who was in dire trouble, but like the magnificent champion he was, he came back to win several of the later rounds and to take referee Arthur Donovan's and the two judges' votes as a points winner. Some idea of how close it was can be gained from the fact that the decision was greeted by loud and long booing. I saw the film of the fight as soon as it reached England, and I have never seen a more hostile reception accorded a verdict in favour of a defending champion. Why, as Louis stood in the centre of the ring, clad in his purple and gold dressing-gown and with both hands raised in victory for the benefit of the Press photographers, there was scarcely a cheer to be heard among the chorus of dissention! Defeat was surely never more glorious than for Farr on this occasion.

Promoter Hulls, through the Boxing Board, had Farr on the mat when he returned home, but this did not disturb the boxer because he had thrown in his lot with Mike Jacobs who had promised him a return with Louis. That would appear to have been his mistake, for his next bout was in the States but against ex-champion Braddock who, though he had retired after being dethroned by Louis, had decided on a comeback. Could this match have been made because Jacobs feared that Farr might have the beating of the champion in a second meeting, and that

the world heavyweight title would thus pass out of his own exclusive control if it landed in the lap of a Briton?

Anyhow, Tommy was talked into taking on Braddock first, and the scheme proved his undoing. Though he seemed to have done enough to win, the stalling tactics of the crafty old-timer kept the issue close, and James J. was given the verdict after which he promptly retired for keeps.

Still Farr refused to come home to defend his British and Empire titles, yet he must have known that there was now no chance of an immediate second meeting with Louis. Instead he gave Max Baer a return in New York, and this time the Tonypandyite found himself well and truly walloped, though his courage won him plenty of plaudits.

Jacobs still gave him fights, but he went down first to Lou Nova and finally to Red Burman who, incidentally, was a protege of Jack Dempsey. That was in January '39, and it meant that Tommy had lost each of five bouts in the States, though he had always been on his feet at the end. To add to his woes, our Board of Control had deprived him of his titles, and Len Harvey had in the meantime beaten Eddie Phillips for the British crown which had been declared vacant.

Before Tommy could so much as step into a ring on his return home, he had to pay a £750 fine which the Board had imposed for his breach of contract over the proposed Schmeling fight. He did this in March '39 and, having patched up the breach

with Hulls, outpointed Red Burman who was brought over for a return clash at Harringay that April. But he wasn't an impressive winner, and several times looked to be in trouble against the left hooking of the American.

After this Tommy beat Larry Gains at Cardiff in May, but it was another disappointing fight with Gains retiring through a damaged hand after five rounds. War came in September, and Farr engaged in only two minor bouts before calling ring warfare a day. He stopped Manuel Abrew in three rounds in Dublin during November, and was too good for Zachy Nicholas at Barnstaple in August 1940. He had enlisted in the Royal Air Force only to be medically discharged.

Blessed with a business brain, Tommy was well fixed financially and for a time all went well in his retirement. He ran a successful public house, and later took over a restaurant which he named 'Tommy Farr's Pantry'. In addition, he had an interest in a successful firm of turf accountants, and he speculated in property. But then his luck ran out.

In the summer of 1950 he announced a comeback--and that after ten years of soft living which must surely have taken their toll. The situation, I think, must have been pretty desperate.

His return to the ring not only helped Tommy out of his financial difficulties, it also put on display once again all the moves of a fistic maestro. Between September 1950, when he re-introduced himself to fight-fans and knocked out Dutchman Jan

Klein in six rounds, and the end of 1952, Tommy took part in fifteen bouts, winning all but four and making most of his opponents look silly. But I was sorry that he had to walk into a 'sucker' punch from Barnoldswick's Frank Bell, for the records now disclose that, for the first time in his life, Tommy was knocked out in the second round at Porth by a man who could scarcely have laid a glove on him ten years earlier.

And of the three adversaries who got the better of him on points, probably only Lloyd Marshall of America would have been allowed to so much as occupy the same ring with him in his heyday. Even so, Tommy looked good enough in action to be paired with Cockell, to decide who should challenge champion Johnny Williams.

Time finally caught up with the lion-hearted Welshman, that night at Nottingham. Against Cockell, Tommy Farr had finally come to the end of the road, for, though the spirit was as willing as ever, the flesh was weak. The Battersea boy, a far better boxer than most folk gave him credit for at that time, outjabbed the man who had been boxing in the booths as a kid before Don himself was born.

After a good start, during which he showed flashes of his former brilliance, it gradually became obvious that the sap was leaving Farr's legs and that the sting was going out of his punches. Being the intelligent fighter that he was, Cockell stepped up the pace and then we knew that if the old warrior did succeed in staying the full twelve rounds course, the best he could hope for was to finish second by a wide points margin.

Despite a sorely wounded eye, Tommy refused to quit and the referee stopped what had become a one-sided bout in the interval after the seventh round. Luckily Farr saw the red light after this battle, and there and then he hung up his gloves for good. It was indeed a tribute to his courage, stamina and skill that, during that enforced comeback, he so often managed to hand out boxing lessons to men fifteen years his junior.

Any comparisons between boxers of different periods must always be invidious, so suffice to say that Tommy Farr came closer to winning the Heavyweight Championship of the World than any other British boxer since old 'Ruby' Bob Fitzsimmons.

After his retirement this Welsh hero lived happily in Shoreham, Sussex, until the final illness which ended his full and active life.

Tommy willed that he should be cremated and his ashes scattered across the Rhondda Valley which he had always loved so dearly.

'Tread light o'er the dead in the valley.....'

CHAPTER SIXTEEN: ROBERT COHEN V. JOHN KELLY; FOR THE BANTAMWEIGHT CHAMPIONSHIP OF EUROPE, IN THE KING'S HALL, BELFAST, ON 27 FEBRUARY, 1954.

The story of John Kelly of Belfast is a tragic one, and it bristles with warnings to boxers potentially of outstanding ability, also to the managers and handlers of such young men. John--no relation to the Derry fighters of the same name, 'Spider' and his sons Billy and Paddy--boxed with his right arm and leg foremost ('southpaw') and was unquestionably one of the most brilliant amateurs that his city has ever produced. He was taught the rudiments of the fistic art in the kitchen of his parents' tiny house in Outram Street.

As a schoolboy he won all the competitions that were open to him, and brought his amateur career to an impressive climax by reaching the final of the featherweight competition in the Milan European Games. There a cut eye robbed him of outright victory--the result of a head-on collison with his French rival.

Now here is the first lesson. When John turned professional, it was decided that he would box in the bantamweight class--a division in which the weight limit is eight pounds lighter than that of the featherweight brigade. As Kelly was still not fully-matured at nineteen years of age, I suggest that this decision, however well-meaning, was an unwise one.

His professional debut took place in December '51, opponent being another former amateur of international repute, Peter Morrison, who hailed from Hull. Kelly, who was under the management of Steve Boyle, a local man who had spent a lifetime in the fight-game, caught the imagination of the Belfast fans right from the start. Indeed, he performed magnificently, for, after out-boxing and out-fighting Morrison, he finished the contest in the sixth round with as workmanlike a knockout as could be wished for.

This win was followed up by successes over such men as Mickey King, Billy Baker, Ron Perry and Jim Dwyer, and so sensational was young John's form that Boyle did not hesitate to match him with brilliant Hogan (Kid) Bassey, then boxing as a bantam but later to prove himself the world's premier nine-stoner.

Many people were of the opinion that this was asking too much of the Irishman, but in spite of their gloomy forebodings Kelly held his own with the coloured fighter and, after eight exciting rounds, he was named the winner in what must have been the equivalent of a photo-finish. This victory, in April 1952, brought the ex-amateur into national prominence but, though offers for his services poured in from all over Britain, he steadfastly refused to fight outside his native city.

Incidentally John, who was them employed as an aircraft fitter, continued to work at his trade in spite of the fact that he looked like reaching the heights as a boxer. I submit that this was mistake number two, and that any boy who aspires to championship calibre in the ring should make the glove-game a full-time occupation.

Success followed success, and Kelly scored thirteen victories in as many starts during 1952, seven of them coming inside the distance. So it went on the next year when, amongst other victims, that brilliant former amateur star, Tommy Proffitt, was demolished in less than two rounds. Eventually John was deemed to be ready for the 'big-time' and, in late June '53, he stopped Eddie 'Bunty' Doran in eleven rounds to win the championship of Northern Ireland.

The way was now clear for a tilt at Peter Keenan's British and European titles, and the bout took place in the King's Hall at the beginning of October. It was a Saturday and, earlier in the day, Scotland had defeated Ireland in a football international; consequently the Scot had plenty of supporters in Belfast who had made the crossing for a real sportsman's day out. They were doomed to disappointment though, for while it was a close affair, with the result in doubt right up to the final bell, tbe Belfast lad won virtually one-handed, jabbing Keenen off balance with right leads and foiling his rival's assaults with some brilliant footwork on the ropes.

When referee Jack Hart raised the local scrapper's hand in victory, the enthusiastic Belfast fans went mad with delight.

Kelly was mobbed in his dressing-room by supporters dancing and some even crying with glee, and now only one person lay between John and a crack at Australian Jimmy Carruthers' world title. This was a swarthy French-Algerian Jewish fighter called Robert Cohen who, after intricate negotiations, agreed to meet Kelly in Belfast providing the latter's European crown was at stake. This fight, which was to prove one of the most tragic episodes that Irish boxing has ever experienced, was clinched by promoter Bob Gardiner to take place in the King's Hall on 27 February 1954, with an almost certain tilt at the world championship as added bait for the winner.

Born at a place called Bone in Algeria on 15 November 1930, Cohen had been boxing professionally for only three months longer than the Irishman but he was some eighteen months older. This would appear to be a matter of no consequence, and in normal circumstances that would indeed be the case.

But Cohen was one of those fighters who had reached maturity early in his career. Perhaps calisthenics and rigorous training schedules had developed his thickset and squat frame particularly rapidly. Kelly, on the other hand, though now past his twenty-second birthday, was one of those lanky lads whose physical development is on the slow side, and who often do not reach full bloom 'till their twenty-fifth or sixth year.

Robert had lost only one out of his thirty-three contests--a points setback which he had subsequently reversed with an inside the distance win. His most recent battle had been waged at Belle Vue, Manchester, the previous December, when he had handed out one hell of a hiding to the South African flyweight, Jake Tuli, to win each of the ten rounds. Earlier he had taken the French crown off the head of Maurice Sandeyron in Paris, and on visiting these shores for the first time had done a terrific demolition job on one of our foremost featherweights, Teddy Peckham from Bournemouth. Peckham, never before stopped inside the distance in nearly a hundred battles, was battered into complete helplessness in six rounds at Belle Vue.

Conceding weight meant little or nothing to the dynamic French-Algerian and, if proof of this other than the Peckham incident be needed, it can be found in the fact that he had also licked class nine-stone men in the persons of Belgium's Jean Sneyers, France's Robert Meunier and Italy's Gaetan Annaloro.

This was an 'all-round' scrapper, for Cohen could both box and fight. Possessed of amazing strength for such a small man, he had a shrewd fighting brain, besides a vicious streak which turned him into a merciless killer whenever he sensed that he had a rival on the run. When Robert went surging from his corner, he would move straight forward, tossing powerful blows at long range, hooking and smashing away at close quarters and treating with scant concern any counters his rivals might hurl back in desperation. If opponents held on for safety, he shoved them hard into the ropes, then went after them with a savage urge to batter them into the canvas. He asked no quarter and gave none, because he was in the ring with one object only--to win.

The continental challenger was obviously in the very peak of condition. After the one o'clock weigh-in--Robert came in just a quarter of a pound inside the stipulated eight stone six--I lunched with him and his handlers at one of Belfast's best hotels. I could hardly believe my eyes as I saw the black-haired Frenchman swill down the whole of a half-bottle of red wine as he disposed of a huge steak and salad. He told me that, at ringtime, he would be much nearer nine stone than eight-six and that he was fortunate to find weight-making no problem, being able to adjust his poundage to within a matter of half-a-stone almost at will. He further said the ingredients of red wine provided him with just the tonic he required on fight-days. Now back to Kelly.

I had my misgivings at the weigh-in which took place on this occasion at the Ulster hall. I had had suspicions all along that John would have a frightful struggle to make the bantamweight limit but, even so, I was quite unprepared to see him looking so finely drawn and pale. Neither did I care for the ugly red blotches that showed in the region of his spine and round his ribs.

He, too, was a quarter of a pound inside the limit but his appearance was in direct contrast to that of the bronzed and clear-eyed Frenchman. Whereas Cohen was bubbling over with vitality, Kelly looked hollow-cheeked and dehydrated. He was silent, almost morose.

A few days previously, I had visited Kelly in his training quarters and was surprised to find him working-out in a dingy, unpainted and bare loft, under conditions which I am forced to say seemed highly unsuitable for a world title prospect. The reason for my trip there was two-fold--firstly I wanted to see what sort of shape the fighter was in, and secondly I was looking for any evidence which might give the lie to my own fears and to the persistent rumours of his experiencing severe weight-difficulties. John only boxed two rounds and he looked great in action against brother Pat. But looking back now, I believe that this was a clue--only two rounds and against his own brother!

Seldom can there have been a fighter so idolised in Ireland as was John Kelly. Even newspapermen could only speak in superlatives, completely disregarding the so-obvious mistakes which he and his advisers were guilty of in the conduct of his affairs. I have since been told that, for a whole week before the Kelly-Cohen bout, there was but a single topic of conversation in the public houses and meeting places of Belfast. Everyone talked about the forthcoming big fight, and how their John would win it.

In the vicinity of Outram Street, where the Kelly family still dwelt, there were huge bonfires stacked ready to celebrate an Irish win, and so repeat the wild scenes of enthusiasm which followed John's triumph over Keenan.

An hour before the doors were due to open, queues began to form outside the hall, and by the time ticket-holders started to arrive it took all one's time to force an entry into the place at all. The fight, if it can be described as such, provided a pitiable spectacle and was a complete anti-climax.

The sound of the opening bell had scarcely died away before the Irishman was pinned on the ropes, taking some battering-ram blows to the midriff. Yet Kelly did not appear unduly perturbed, and the crowd roared when he jabbed Cohen off with his right and then followed up with a left cross to the jaw. Neither of these blows disturbed the Frenchman in the least, and immediately he came boring in again. As John neatly side-stepped his man on the ropes, Robert accidentally caught the champion under the chin with his head, for which he was spoken to by referee Gilardi of Italy at the end of the session.

If Cohen had appeared menacing up to this point, scarcely anyone could have visualised the sensations that were to follow. The Frenchman began the second with a rush as, ducking Kelly's right lead, he forced the Irish boy backwards across the ring throwing powerful punches with incredible rapidity.

Almost before John had raised his gloves, a cascade of blows crashed against his unguarded jaw and a right hook dropped him to the boards for a count of four. Mouth agape and badly hurt, Kelly rose to face an adversary who, exhilarated with success, was now fighting with almost demoniacal fury. Again the Irishman collapsed and again he failed to take anything like the full respite allowed, climbing to his feet at 'three'. But the Italian referee, abiding by the rules as then practised only in his own country, none the less continued to count to 'eight' before giving the order to 'box on'.

Straightaway Kelly was laid low again by a short right to the chin, and it could only have been the instinctive urge possessed by all real fighters which enabled him to drag himself to his feet at 'six', for he was undoubtedly badly concussed. With another bombardment of savagely delivered blows, Cohen again dropped the sorely battered Irish fighter, who was now nothing more than a wide-open and sitting target.

It seemed to be all over, but, with almost unbelievable courage, the Belfast boxer forced himself erect at 'nine' only to be felled again by a right which landed simultaneously with the clang of the bell to end the round. Kelly crashed forward on his face, and there can be no doubt whatsoever that he was utterly unconscious. As his seconds dragged him to his corner, it could be seen that the right side of Kelly's face was grazed and spotted with the resin dust off the floor of the ring.

Here an observation of my own. To this day I cannot understand why Kelly's handlers were allowed to carry their unconscious principal to the corner. More than a year previously, a similar incident had occurred in an eliminator for the featherweight title between Freddie King of Walworth and Tommy Miller of Scotland in London. That was a twelve-rounder and, towards the end of the eleventh, King was miles ahead on points. He was then knocked out cold, only for the bell to come to his rescue at 'eight'.

The late Frank Duffett, one of King's seconds, dragged him to his corner and was able to revive him sufficiently to enable him to last out the final session and so win on points. This caused the Board of Control to issue an instruction soon afterwards which decreed that any boxer prostrate on the canvas yet saved by the bell must not be carried to his corner. I can only conclude that, because the count had not actually started in the case of Kelly, the action of his seconds was tolerated.

But be that as it may, I am firmly convinced that he should not have been allowed to answer the bell for the third round, even though desperate work in the interval had partially restored his faculties. With blank eyes and tottering legs, John staggered to the centre of the ring and even managed to summon up a couple of weak swings. Then over came Cohen's right, bang on target, and down went Ireland's gallant son for the last time.

The count was nothing more than a formaility, but at 'six' the towel came fluttering in from Kelly's corner. This is no longer a legitimate signal of surrender, so, rightly, referee Gilardi ignored it and continued counting Kelly out.

This defeat robbed him of all confidence in his fistic ability, and he never again showed more than a flash of the brilliance of his early days in the roped arenas. He took a short rest, then undertook a comeback bout against the seasoned Belgian, Pierre Cossemyns. After a good beginning, all the strength and zip suddenly seemed to leave John, and he was dropped for the full count in the ninth as the result of a punch wihch did not look over-powerful.

After a further five months' rest, he was called on to defend his British title against the man from whom he had won it, Peter Keenan. The fight took place in Paisley, Scotland, which meant that Kelly was boxing away from home for the first time and, as I have described in another chapter, he was knocked out in the sixth round of a 'one-horse race'.

Nobody really knows what went wrong with Kelly, but personally I believe that the strain of weight-making extinguished for good the vital spark of genius that was so noticeable in the early part of his career. Yet he has always insisted that eight stone six was his best fighting weight and, when he tried again as a featherweight in 1955, he looked far from impressive in two winning bouts and was knocked out in the first round by Teddy

Peckham in Belfast during the late summer. His final appearance as an active ringman was in May 1957 and, as usual, in Belfast. Then he made terribly hard work of beating a very mediorcre nine-stone performer, Teddy Barker from Swindon, and that spelt 'finis'.

Seven months after vanquishing Kelly, Robert Cohen went on to capture the vacant world championship (Carruthers had retired in the meantime) by outpointing Chamrern Songkitrat in Bangkok. He reigned supreme among the bantamweights until late June 1956 when Mario D'Agata, the Italian deaf-mute, forced him to retire in six rounds. As a matter of interest, his win made D'Agata the first deaf-mute in boxing history to win a world title. Cohen announced his retirement from active combat on 10 July that year.

The Cohen-Kelly fight story, then, is the tale of two men of equal fistic standing who clashed in a fight brought about by the natural sequence of events in the ring. But what should, on paper, have been a close and thrilling battle was instead the beginning of the end for the Irishman.

For Cohen the immediate future held only great triumph; for Kelly only decline and fall.

CHAPTER SEVENTEEN: ROCKY MARCIANO V. DON COCKELL; FOR THE HEAVYWEIGHT CHAMPIONSHIP OF THE WORLD, IN THE KEZAR STADIUM, SAN FRANCISCO, ON 16 MAY, 1955.

Not since Tommy Farr went the distance with Joe Louis at New York's Yankee Stadium, in August, 1937, had Britain so much as offered a challenge for boxing's crown of crowns, the World Heavyweight Championship, when Don Cockell stepped in with Rocky Marciano. Indeed, right from the time when glove fights were first instituted only six of our pugilists, apart from Bob Fitzsimmons, who annexed the title in 1897, had contested the issue.

First, Birmingham's Charlie Mitchell failed against James J. Corbett, then, when Tommy Burns visited Britain as reigning champion at the end of 1907, he undertook three defences in the space of three months, two of them being in London and the other in Dublin. First the champion KO'd the reigning British kingpin, Gunner Moir, in ten rounds, then former titleholder, Jack Palmer in four. In Ireland he disposed of Jem Roche in half-a-round and also accounted for another British fighter, Jewey Smith, in Paris. During more than twenty-nine years which passed before Tommy Farr got his chance, thirty contests involving the big championship were fought without a British challenger being concerned, while there were no fewer than forty between that time and the date of the Marciano-Cockell fight.

Only guts, determination and faith won Cockell his crack at the title. The critics had said he was on the way out when he was stopped by the American negro, Jimmy Slade, back in December 1951, and they announced that he was all washed-up when Randolph Turpin deprived him of his lightheavyweight crowns in June 1952.

What they didn't know was that Don was going through torture in his efforts to keep down to twelve stone seven. Each day he boiled off pound after pound, only to find that his weight was increasing just the same. He dieted, consulted specialists, but all in vain. So, at last, he decided to let nature take its course and box as a heavyweight.

Although he stopped Paddy Slavin on his debut, the experts just laughed at him. 'He's too slow and fat', they said. 'He'd do better to pack it in altogether'. No more favourable notices were posted when he followed up by walloping the hard-punching schoolmaster, Frank Bell, and even an inside-the-distance victory over Tommy Farr in a heavyweight title eliminator brought scant praise. They said that Tommy was years past his best, and should never have attempted a comeback. But when, in May '53, Cockell took the British and Empire heavyweight titles off the head of clever Johnny Williams, everyone suddenly realised that here was a British heavyweight who could really fight.

Between that date and the end of July '54, Cockell stormed into action six times. He performed the hat-trick over the American, Harry Matthews--two of these being gained in Matthews' home town of Seattle. As famous manager Jack Hurley had been shouting the American's praises from the rooftops, Don's performances placed him to the fore of the challengers for Marciano's title. More especially as the international element proves a particularly big lure at the gate for championship fights in the United States.

Don's other wins came over Italian Uber Bacillieri in Leicester, a successful Johannesburg defence of his Empire laurels against the South African champion, Johnny Arthur, and a Harringay verdict over Roland LaStarza, the American 'College Boy'. As LaStarza, only six months previously, had gone nearly eleven rounds with Marciano and given him plenty of trouble into the bargain, the British kingpin's stock was indeed high. When the match with the world champion was made, Don was unbeaten for almost three years and was certainly the most popular boxer in Britain.

At Sleaford Street School, in Battersea, they told him he was too big for boxing, so instead he took up Soccer. As a centre-half with the Cadet Force, he shone. But, fortunately, in the boxing championships there were weight classes for the bigger and heavier boys. Soon he won the National Army Cadet Force title and began to carve out a promising career with the

Caius Amateur Club. In 1946, he was beaten by Len Fowler in the final of the London ABA championships.

A blacksmith by trade, Cockell wasn't earning sufficient to get married so he went to the premises that were, in those days, Jack Solomons' gymnasium, and asked permission to spar with middleweight Vince Hawkins. His form so impressed the late John Simpson , Hawkins' manager, that he agreed to manage the Battersea boy and they remained together throughout Cockell's ring career.

Don earned himself £8 for beating Trevor Lowder on 26 June 1946, in his pro' debut, while for the Marciano bout he received well in excess of £23,000. What happened in between can be gauged from the fact that he had, in all, seventy-five contests, all but nine of them around the lightheavyweight limit. Of these he lost eleven, including the Slade and Turpin setbacks which I mentioned earlier.

He won the British cruiserweight title in October '50, added the European crown the following March and defended both honours successfully by knocking out Albert Finch of Croydon in seven rounds in October 1951. This, then, was the cockney about to attempt to become the first British-born heavyweight to win the World crown since Fitzsimmons.

When, in 1952, Rocky Marciano became the first white heavyweight champion since 1937, he also set up a record. With an unbroken string of forty-three victories, he became the first

heavyweight ruler to win the title without first suffering either a setback or a draw. Yet he was licked as an amateur, Coley Wallace, Joey De Angeles and Ted Lester being his conquerors. On the day he met Cockell, his record read forty-seven wins in as many battles, with only seven opponents lasting the full distance.

There was not a lot of boxing about Rocky. He just waded in to belt them left, right and centre and when he caught his rivals fair and square they never failed to hit the deck. Marciano's childhood was tough, and so he became the tough-guy of the roped square. Not elsewhere, though, for he was a modest, gentle fellow with a sense of humour and a generous heart.

Born Rocko Francis Marchegiano and one of a large family of impoverished Italian immigrants, Marciano knew only the hard way from birth. He was fighting for existence in Brockton, Mass., almost as soon as he learned to walk, and it didn't take him long to realise that, among his personal assets, strength would have to be number one priority.

When he was in England as a G.I. during the later stages of the last war, he was in a tavern with some of his friends when a giant Australian threatened to push his face in. Marciano's response was a wild right-uppercut--later to become famous as his 'Susie-Q' blow--that stretched the Aussie out cold. Rocky, by the way, was drinking a Coca-Cola as he always did, and he was

quite shocked to learn later that he had put the skids under the champion heavyweight of the Australian Overseas Forces!

After his discharge, he decided to commercialise his fists and set out on the road to the top in February 1947. After twenty-two victories, most of them in Providence, they put him in the Madison Square Garden ring and he was a sensation, winning in two rounds.

His second appearance there saw him in opposition to a hard-punching New York fighter called Carmine Vingo. Vingo set out to knock Marciano cold and, in the fifth round, he hit him with the hardest blow he had ever received, a crushing right to the chin. Only Marciano's tremendous resilience and power of recuperation enabled him to beat the count, yet he came back like a wounded animal, out to make a kill. Vingo was blasted unconscious in the sixth with the 'Susie-Q', and he was at death's door for ten days with a fractured skull, concussion of the brain and partial paralysis. Carmine was told that he must never box again and Rocky sent a cheque for $2,000 to help pay hospital expenses, following up with another $500 to help his rival get started in some new way of earning a living.

That was at the end of 1949, yet the sportswriters slated the new Brockton sensation as 'a crude operator who can hit, but has no other visible assets'. They maintained this view even after 1951, the year when he tangled with the great Joe Louis, who

was making the inevitable comeback. Joe had won eight fights in a row and he thought Marciano would make it nine.

There can be no doubt, of course, that Louis was miles past his best at this time. Yet the fact is that the old 'Bomber' was so intent on watching the danger in Rocky's right, that he overlooked the left. This caught him with stunning force in the eighth to send him through the ropes too dazed to climb back before 'out' had been called.

Marciano treated Lee Savold and a couple of others in similar fashion, and then they matched him with the aforementioned Harry Matthews who, at that time, boasted an unbeaten run of nearly fifty outings. That bout took place in July 1952 and it cleared the way for Marciano to meet Jersey Joe Walcott for the championship. He finished Matthews in the second round with a left hook, followed by that dynamite-charged right swing-cum uppercut.

Two months later Rocky was world champion, for he stopped Walcott in the thirteenth round after he himself had been completely outboxed during the early stages of the contest. Eight months after this, he KO'd Jersey Joe in one round in the return, and followed this up by stopping LaStarza in the last week of September '53.

Still the experts insisted that Marciano could only punch, but, in June '54, he outpointed polished Ezzard Charles over fifteen rounds to finally silence his critics. Then, in September,

he made doubly certain by knocking the same opponent out in the eighth round of a return.

A few days before the Marciano-Cockell clash, there was scarcely an American in the States who conceded the British fighter any real chance of success. Indeed, in this country there were precious few who had any firm optimistic convictions about Cockell's chances, and I readily confess that I was not among those few!

We all knew Don to be a biding and resourceful box-fighter, one who knew all the moves and could take care of himself in tight corners, for he had nine years experience behind him during which time he had suffered only the barest physical damage. At twenty-six, too, he was the younger man by four years. But, I argued, he had met with defeat on more than one occasion while the world champion, crude and unorthodox as he might be, had yet to meet his master and it was he who packed by far the heavier dig.

I felt certain that Cockell did not carry the heavy armoury necessary to put the American on the canvas, but I hoped he might bamboozle Rocky sufficiently to stay the full course and so could just possibly sneak a points verdict.

On the other hand, Marciano had been most surprisingly dumped on the seat of his pants during a sparring session by a coloured partner called Toxie Hall, and this had aroused a faint feeling of doubt oncerning the invincibility of the 'Brockton

Blockbuster's' chin. This, allied to his known susceptibility to cuts, gave rise to further optimism on the part of Cockell rooters--more especially as the Londoner, the man one American writer had the temerity to say 'would louse up our town' when the match was first announced, had been displaying tremendous form in his final workouts after initially being unimpressive. And at the weigh-in Don had scaled 14 stone nine as against Marciano's 13 stone seven.

The British champion was first into the ring, wearing a blue woollen robe over black shorts, with a broad white stripe down either leg. Marciano appeared wearing a black dressing-gown with red embroidery, his name and home town emblazoned in bold letters on the back. It was not by chance that his trunks were in the exact opposite colours to those worn by Cockell, for it is a practice in the States to make the boxers easily recognisable even to those in the far-off seats--and a highly commendable practice it is, too.

Now to the fight itself. Today there is no blinking the fact that Rocky Marciano was one of the truly great World Heavyweight Champions. He overcame our man by sheer weight of punching-power and bull-dozing aggression, by accepting the best and hardest blows that Cockell could throw at him and never ceasing to move forward to toss his own mighty punches.

Yet those who imagined that the fight would be a fiasco; that Don would be bludgeoned into unconsciousness in a round

or so, were made to eat their words. As it happened, Rocky was denied even the satisfaction of scoring a knockout, though he had the challenger down at the end of the eighth and floored him twice early in the ninth. But Don was still on his feet when the referee called a halt.

True, he could not have lasted much longer, though he was prepared to fight on to the bitter end. Our champion gave a thrilling exhibition of true British pluck and, although defeated, was certainly not disgraced.

Cockell won the first two rounds through his better boxing, but there was insufficient weight behind his blows to check the iron-muscled Marciano. Rocky bored in, fists flying, with follow-through smashes from wrists, forearms, elbows and shoulders. It was the only way he knew how to fight, though, with a British referee, he would never have been allowed to get away with such tactics. He crashed his way through the British champion's defence and, although Don rode dozens of punches in every round, he could not avoid them all.

As expected, our man made the world champion miss badly at times, but failure to hit the target neither worried nor inconvenienced Marciano. As one mighty blow swept the empty air, he was dispatching a second with his other arm. In America this is known as 'combination punching', but Cockell must have thought that he was fighting a belligerent octopus.

It seemed that Don's plan was to use a left jab and ride Rocky's counters. He did this successfully for the first two rounds, but Marciano stepped up the pace to such an extent that Cockell was compelled to stand toe-to-toe and swap blows. While these may have been mistaken tactics, they were also unavoidable. The world champion was not prepared to allow the brawl to develop into a boxing match, for he was in there with the fixed intention of knocking his rival out of the proceedings in the shortest possible time.

Against this rough-house slugging, scientific boxing was swept aside. Cockell gave ground when forced to do so, but he seemed to prefer to stand firm and trade punches. This was, of course, almost akin to fistic suicide and, though he held his own for a time, he could make no impression on the champion no matter how hard or where he hit him. On the other hand, Rocky's sledgehammer shots began to make noticeable effect after four rounds, especially some of those to the body which were borderline in their proximity to being 'low'.

At the first signs of the Londoner's weariness, Marciano became even more ferocious and Cockell must have been in superb shape to have kept his feet under such a murderous battering. He endured severe punishment in the fifth, but came back fighting in the next session and caused a great roar to go up as he crossed the champion with a magnificent right to the chin.

For the merest second, the American was pulled up short, but then the avalanche swept forward again and Cockell had to fight back with all the force at his command to prevent himself from being submerged. That was almost the end of Don's gallant resistance. In the seventh and eighth his defences were down and at the end of the latter session he looked all-in. No one would have blamed him if he had not answered the bell for the ninth.

But Cockell knew that thousands of his well-wishers were following the round-by-round radio commentary of the battle back home in England--It was by now about 3.45a.m. here--and he strode forth to meet his doom in the ninth.

Marciano was on him like a flash and, although Cockell valiantly tried to fight him off, he now had nothing left to offer. Down for 'seven', he pulled himself off the canvas only to go crashing down again as 'The Rock' tagged him on the chin. This time Don rose too quickly, probably because he was so badly dazed. He staggered backwards and, after he had taken two further mighty blows, referee Frankie Brown mercifully put an end to what was becoming a slaughter. The final round had lasted only fifty-four seconds.

After the contest, both men spoke through the ring microphone. Marciano said: 'I have never fought a tougher boy than Don. Walcott, Charles and Louis all took plenty from me, but nobody I ever fought took more than the limey. I hit him

something awful, but he's a great guy and very much underrated. Britain should be proud of her Don Cockell'.

Cockell was accorded a tremendous ovation after speaking, for he said simply; 'I am disappointed, because I really thought I was going to win. I just hope I haven't let anybody down'.

And here are a few newspaper quotes on the subject of Don's courage..... 'he fought to the last gasp....' 'no gamer man ever stepped into a boxing ring....' 'gave everything he had against Rocky's rough-house tactics....' 'fought like a lion against odds that were just too great for him....'

I now quote from the late Eamonn Andrews' radio commentary; 'Marciano is one of the toughest champions who ever rubbed a foot in resin. But he never read the rule books, and he had a different version of the sport from the one Cockell was taught. He butted with the head, used his elbows, hit low and hit after the bell. A British referee would have sent him to his corner after three rounds'.

On 27 April the following year, Rocky called a Press Conference to announce his retirement. He was the second scrapper to quit the game as undefeated World Heavyweight Champion--and stay retired. The other, of course, being Gene Tunney.

Marciano remained undefeated in forty-nine contests, including six title defences and he was, as far as it is possible to

trace, one of only four professional fighters of any calibre who went through their entire ring career unbeaten. I can think of no finer tribute to his prowess.

He died in an aircrash in Iowa on 31 August, 1969.

CHAPTER EIGHTEEN: HOGAN (KID) BASSEY V. CHERIF HAMIA; FOR THE FEATHERWEIGHT CHAMPIONSHIP OF THE WORLD, IN THE PALAIS DES SPORTS, PARIS, ON 24 JUNE, 1957.

The retirement of Sandy Saddler in January 1957 gave France a chance of regaining the world's featherweight title which she had last held through Andre Routis in 1929. And the man who had the opportunity of bringing home the bacon was Cherif Hamia, a twenty-six year old Algerian, who had won the European crown eight days previously in a bout with Belgium's Jean Sneyers.

Cherif was unanimously selected by all the leading controlling bodies in the world to meet the winner of two eliminators for the world championship, the other contenders named being Miguel Berrios of Puerto Rico, America's Carmelo Costa and our own Hogan (Kid) Bassey from Nigeria.

In the spring of 1956, the French-Algerian had visited the United States and in three storming bouts had defeated both Costa and Berrios, together with another leading nine-stone man in the person of Ike Chestnut. Little wonder, then, that all France felt certain that in Hamia they had the successor to Saddler, and Cherif himself had every reason for feeling that way.

Like all French members of the boxing fraternity, he idolised the memory of the late great Marcel Cerdan, the French middleweight who carried the world title home from America, then lost it and was killed in an air crash on the way back to the United States in an effort to regain it for his country.

Hamia was only a boy when Cerdan was fighting, but it was always his ambition to emulate him. The Algerian's first visit to the United States was a fleeting one in 1953, when he competed against a Golden Gloves team and won his bout. On that occasion he spent a couple of days each in Chicago and New York.

It was while he was performing with credit in the French amateur ranks that Cherif was spotted by manager Philippe Filippi, who handled the affairs of such top-class performers as Charles Humez and Alphonse Halimi. Hamia's family were very much against him fighting for a living and his father's ambition was for his son to follow in his own footsteps as a mason. Hamia studied pharmacy before he turned professional--a trade which stood him in good stead when his boxing days finished.

Soon after signing professional forms, his manager brought him to Paris, where he soon ran up a long string of victories, most of them being gained inside the distance. Within twelve months he had won fifteen bouts, including one which gained him the French title by stopping Jacques Dumesnil in ten rounds, together with successes over the two talented Italians, Altidora Polidori and Aldo Pravisani. Then followed an unexpected setback--a kayo defeat against Belgian Louis Cabo, and that in the first round, too, during December '54.

But then Cherif got back to winnning vein and, in December '55, he showed his undoubted class by stopping Robert Cohen, the then world bantamweight champion, in ten rounds in Paris. Although an overweight match, this reverse must have had a great effect on Cohen, for he fought only once more before retiring. There followed a drawn bout with Jean Sneyers, and the American trip which I described earlier.

He surprised the sportswriters in the States by the intensity of his training, for the accent was on speed the whole time. Against Carmelo Costa, at Madison Square Garden, the Frenchman had to be content with a split-decision, after staggering his opponent in the second, third and eighth rounds. Hamia then gained a majority verdict over Chestnut in Washington.

His third bout, against Berrios, marked his best performance. Cherif had become well acclimatised by then, and he won a unanimous victory, besides putting his opponent on the canvas in the fourth session. Millions of television fans from coast-to-coast saw this one.

Before Hamia left America for home, Harry Markson, managing director of the Internationsl Boxing Club, told him: 'You've earned a world title shot under heavy fire, and we'll begin immediate negotiations for you to meet champion Sandy Saddler. It should be a big draw'.

Well, it is now history how Saddler was involved in a car crash soon after this and that he decided to hang up his gloves for good. And so it was only right and proper that Hamia should be one of the contestants in a bout for the championship he had vacated.

Berrios beat Costa in the first series eliminator. Then, as we shall see a little later, Bassey outscored the Puerto Rican to earn the right to occupy the opposite corner to Hamia in a title match at the Palais Des Sports in Paris in mid-summer, 1957.

In a warm-up fight at the end of April in Montreal--in point of fact it took place just four days after Bassey licked Berrios--Hamia gave a dazzling display of speed and left hand work to outpoint the much thought-of American, Bobby Bell. This was just the sort of battle he needed to tune him up for the Bassey encounter, for Bell proved himself a snappy counter-puncher and, although he could not match the Frenchman for speed, Bobby was in fine physical condition and the exchanges were always interesting.

So, when he stepped in with Bassey, the Frenchman had engaged in thirty-three professional bouts, of which he had won thirty-one and had boxed one draw.

Bassey was born in Creek Town, Calabar, on 3 June 1932. At school he had only one ambition--to study hard and one day become an engineer. He went to Lagos to live with an aunt in the hope of getting a better education, but it didn't work out like that and he eventually moved to the house of an uncle who ran a boxing club for the youth of the city. That was where curly-haired Hogan first donned the gloves and, by the time he was sixteen, he had turned professional. A year later he won the Nigerian flyweight title by outpointing a boxer by the colourful name of Dick Turpin. In 1950 he added the Nigerian bantamweight crown, and in 1951 the West African eight stone six championship.

A Yorkshire business man, Mr. Jack Farnsworth, saw this feat performed, and he offered to pay Bassey's fare to England. Thus it was that he arrived at Liverpool that December, full of ambition and bubbling over with excitement.

On 31 January 1952 he had his first fight at Liverpool Stadium. It was against a lad called Ray Hilliard, and Hogan won in the fourth round--an achievement which naturally delighted him. He went into action as a bantamweight no less than nineteen times that year, emerging as the loser on only three occasions and boxing in such places as Manchester, Leeds, Belfast, Hanley and West Hartlepool.

Things were going well now and, after licking the European bantamweight kingpin, Luis Romero, the next February, Hogan found himself in the forefront of our eight-stone-six men.

But weight-making for that division was becoming a burden, so Bassey decided to throw his cap among the featheweights. He walloped Denny Dawson and Tommy Higgins in quick succession, but was then adjudged the loser against Juan Alvarez in Newcastle in what was one of the most incomprehensible decisions i have ever seen rendered. I thought the Nigerian clearly won every single round.

About this time Bassey was experiencing difficulty in obtaining opponents, and there was a £500 challenge out on his behalf to any man in the country. The backers of Sammy McCarthy took this up, only to see their man narrowly outpointed after a classic encounter. That win should have put 'The Kid' in line for a crack at Roy Ankrah's Empire title, but in his final contest of the year he dropped a verdict to Belfast's Billy Kelly in London.

When Hogan licked European champion Jean Sneyers in April '54 he was right back in the picture, but then, in the midst of six winning bouts, came a setback against a lesser Belgian called Jo Woussem. He seemed to be jinxed to fail just when he got within easy reach of real glory.

Kelly had deprived Ankrah of the title in October '54, and Bassey was certain that he was the Irishman's master, even though he had been on the wrong end of the verdict in their only meeting. By the time Hogan had run up a further three victories during the early part of 1955, Kelly was ordered to put the title on the line against the persistent Nigerian, who went into action victoriously, twice more, before he opposed Billy in the King's Hall, Belfast, on 19 November.

A clash of heads caused a bad injury to Bassey's eye in the fifth round and, at the end of the seventh, the referee examined the wound before deciding that he could allow the Nigerian just one more round in which to attempt to snatch victory. Realising that now it was all or nothing, Hogan caught his rival with a perfect short right in the eighth and knocked him out. At long last he was Empire champion! Yet, even so, plenty of troubles lay ahead.

Strangely, Bassey has disclosed that 1956 was far from being a happy year for him. He engaged in six bouts, but they were for comparatively small purses and, up to October, he was in dire financial straits. He actually got a job learning to be a motor-mechanic, because, to make finance more important to him still, his wife was expecting a child.

Nevertheless, after a most worrying time during which he seriously contemplated quitting the ring altogether, his business affairs were taken over by George Biddles of Leicester. This was just about the finest thing that ever happened to Bassey, for Biddles pressed his charge's claims for a crack at higher honours to the British Boxing Board of Control, even before the news of Sandy Saddler's retirement had been received. He gave Bassey new enthusiasm for the fight-game.

The Board backed Bassey, and all of a sudden he found himself with too many fights on his hands. Nominated to oppose Berrios in a final eliminator in Washington, Hogan was also called on to go through with a defence of his Empire title against Percy Lewis in Nottingham, twenty-five days earlier.

After meeting and beating Lewis, he found Berrios comparatively easy meat and allowed his rival to win only one round out of twelve. Popular Miguel was made favourite in the pre-fight betting, but he found himself left-hooked as he had never been left-hooked before. It proved a good fight to watch, and was an excellent build-up to the contest for the world title. Berrios adopted his usual swinging tactics, but Hogan had never boxed better and never relaxed his grip on the bout. At close quarters he was always the master.

His win meant that Nigeria got the chance of winning her first world boxing championsip at any weight, and it also meant that Britain came into the picture with the prospect of having a world featherweight titleholder for the first time since 1920. In that year Tommy Noble of Bermondsey won promoter Tex Rickard's Diamond Belt, which was in those days emblematic of the world title, though it must be conceded that a far better qualified claimant to the throne at that time was Johnny Kilbane.

Other interesting facts about the Bassey-Hamia pairing are that it marked the first occasion in the history of the division when the world nine stone championship was competed for by two non-Americans, and that it was over seven years since a fighter other than an American had so much as boxed in the role

of challenger, Frenchman Ray Famechon having been the last, back in March 1950.

Bassey disembarked in Paris a week before the bout, in order that he might have sufficient time to get acclimatised to the city before the great day dawned. Nobody in Paris seemed to give the Nigerian much chance of winning and, at the weigh-in, Hamia was so hotly fancied that there was scarely any wagering--though there was plenty of real French enthusiasm!

Hamia fans screamed themselves hoarse as the confident, cocksure Cherif smiled his way through the preliminaries. Dead on the weight limit of nine stone, he was a pound and six ounces heavier than Bassey, and he had an advantage of two inches in reach and three in height.

That he was seldom able to use them to his benefit or, for that matter, his fleet-footedness, speaks volumes for the fashion in which the Liverpool-domiciled Nigerian went to work. Rarely did Bassey make a mistake. In fact, the only real one I can recall came when he ran into a right-hander in the second round. And, as should happen in a fight between the world's top men, he had to pay by being on the receiving end of the hardest blow he had ever taken in his life.

He was hurt, make no mistake about that. But the supreme fitness and wonderful condition into which his trainer, Charlie Fox, had worked him, paid off handsome dividends. Hogan rose at 'seven', dazed and weak. After taking another solid

jab, his fighting brain ordered him to fight back--and fight back he did. Excellent advice from the corner sent him out to box his way back to confidence in the third, and Hogan obeyed his advisers implicitly.

From the fourth round onwards Bassey treated us to a fine display of left-hand work, shuffling and feinting his way in to make the Frenchman feel the maximum effect of his jabs, and digging in his left hooks to the body for good measure. By the end of that session the man who had looked all over a winner was beginning to blow and his features were already noticeably disfigured.

Soon there were unmistakable signs that the snap was going from Hamia. His counters made sounds when they landed to indicate so obviously that he was slapping, and the Empire champion went through his punching repertoire with vicious hooks to the body, his most important stock-in-trade.

Half-way through the sixth Cherif's right eye was split and bleeding, and he spent most of the next round taking evasive action. The eighth saw the Frenchman getting very few blows through Bassey's watertight guard, one or other of Hogan's mobile hands catching Hamia's punches from the cross-armed position so characteristic of the compact Nigerian. And as he thwarted his rival's best efforts, Hogan still sank in those pile-drivers to the midsection.

The crowd was almost silent in the ninth, sensing impending disaster for their cherished idol. Every time Hamia tried to set himself to throw a weighty blow, Basey clipped him with a left hook to the head. He pummelled Cherif on the ropes with a furious, two-handed assault, and when the continental boy tried to fight his way out of trouble, the coloured terror merely repeated the process.

Hamia left his corner for a 'last-ditch' effort in the tenth round. He put everything he had into a do-or-die attempt, but Bassey simply scorned his punches. Then, suddenly, he spotted THE opening. The once-handsome Hamia's hands were getting lower and lower all the time, and now his jaw appeared--all unprotected and inviting.

A short left, and Hamia was on his way staggering backwards towards the Nigerian's corner. A long swinging right-hander helped him on his way. 'The Kid' pounced--bang, bang! The punches rained on the hapless European champion, who seemed to decide that if he was going to the boards, then he would take his adversary there with him.

He grabbed the coloured boy by the legs, and down they went in a heap, Bassey, on top, quickly struggling free.Somehow Hamia got up, too, and moved along the ropes away from Bassey, who, tigerlike, pounced on him again. Once more the punches descended on him in a hail of concentrated fury and, as Hamia slipped lower and lower over the middle rope, his legs

gone, the last dregs of resistance sapped, the merciful arms of referee Schemann halted the bout with two minutes twenty-nine seconds of the round gone.

Hamia had been beaten into a shambling, helpless hulk, and the referee's only alternative to terminating the proceedings would have been to allow the Algerian to be driven clean through the canvas.

That contest provided everything that one could wish for in excitement and drama, not to mention an able demonstration of the boxing skills by two fine exponents, together with the kind of punching-power one expects to see in a world title bout.

And, to cap it all, Hogan proved that he was stamped in the mould of true champions by getting up off the floor to win--and that from a blow that would have spelt defeat for a lesser gladiator.

The French speedster was outspeeded by sheer 'black magic' and ringcraft and, having outboxed and clearly out-thought his man, Bassey finished his task in a blaze of punching-glory which left even the partisan 18,000 odd capacity crowd stunned by its ferocity and expediency.

At the ringside, it looked as if the world title bout was going to start all over again. The Algerians were not happy that their man had lost, and one of the Nigerian Ministers who was in Paris to watch the fight got a black eye!

Bassey supporters leapt into the ring to carry him round shoulder high. They were laughing, crying, shouting and jumping. And why not? For we had our first world champion for almost six years.

I would add that Hogan (Kid) Bassey, Gentleman of the Roped Square, was awarded the M.B.E. in the 1958 New Year's Honours List--the first boxer to be so recognised.

CHAPTER NINETEEN: ELLSWORTH 'SPIDER' WEBB V. TERRY DOWNES, TEN ROUNDS MIDDLEWEIGHT CONTEST AT 11 STONE 8 POUNDS AT THE EMPIRE POOL, WEMBLEY ON 9 DECEMBER, 1958.

On 25 January 1957, our party in the Punch Tavern in Fleet Street was joined by Terry Downes and his father. I was particularly pleased to see them for, only twenty-four hours earlier, they had arrived home on the Queen Mary, after spending four years in the United States. I had met young Downes before his departure for America, and I remembered seeing him as a member of the Pembroke Amateur Boxing Club in Paddington, outpointed in the ABA Youth title final by the long-since retired midlands lightweight, Harry Edwards.

Some four years previously, Downes' sister, a trapeze artiste, had been badly injured in a circus accident in the States and her parents decided to visit her. They took sixteen-yearold Terry along with them and no sooner had they arrived in Baltimore when he joined the local Y.M.C.A. to become the terror of the boxing section.

Anxious to keep their members, it was suggested to Downes that he might like to join the U.S. Marines, about the toughest bunch of fighting servicemen that America produces. He promptly signed on for three years.

There he got the toughening-up treatment that served him so well in the ring. He also became Welterweight Champion of the Marines and, eventually, the All-Services titleholder. They even selected him to represent the United States in the 1956 Olympic Games at Melbourne, until it was discovered that he was of British birth. According to the only records at hand, he took part in eighty-three bouts there altogether, losing only five and winning inside the distance in no less than thirty-two occasions.

Because Terry beat America's Olympic representative, Pearce Lane, as well as the man whom Lane licked in the Trials final, the critics dubbed the English boy the 'Amateur Welterweight Champion of America'.

Now that he was back in England, Terry told me, he wanted above all to win an ABA championship. While in America he had read all about the exploits of the famous Fisher Catholic Club down in Bermondsey with which I was connected, and so I arranged for him to join that first-class outfit.

His first appearance in their colours was sensational, to say the least. Displaying the typical American all-action style, Downes mowed down his opponent, Bill Robinson from Brixton, in little more than a round. But soon after this Terry was booked to box at Seymour Hall, Marylebone, on a show jointly sponsored by the Polytechnic and St. Pancras Clubs. His opponent, however, failed to show up and Downes eventually gave away what some said was twelve pounds to an Army Private called

Albert Adanolfi. But I knew that, in fact, Downes conceded nearer a stone-and-a-half than twelve pounds for he stepped on the scales fully dressed, and with his clenched fists loaded with copper coins. This was because, had he been content to come in at his natural poundage, he would have certainly been prevented from going through with the contest by well-meaning officials.

Downes was well on top in the second round when he received a slight abrasion, about an inch above the forehead, one which had begun to bleed slightly. Without hesitation, the referee stopped the bout and awarded the decision to Adanolfi.

It seemed very harsh treatment on Downes, who was thus stopped for the first time in seven years' boxing. When I walked into the dressing-room after the contest, Downes was surrounded by a crowd of angry supporters: there was no trace of a wound.

I had to inquire as to the exact whereabouts of the injury and Terry pulled back his hair to reveal a slight scratch. He was boiling over with rage--which I could well understand--and he told me, there and then, that he was disgusted with English amateur boxing and that he would in future fight as a professional. The likeable Terry had made a host of friends among the Fisher Club's supporters and, though it meant forfeiting what looked like a certain ABA title for their Club, Club

officials heartily endorsed the boxer's decision in his own interests.

And so it came to pass that on 9 April 1957, Terry made his professional debut at Harringay on the bill in which Dave Charnley captured the national lightweight title off Joe Lucy. Downes was matched with the hard-hitting and experienced Peter Longo, but poor Peter was counted out after only ninety seconds of the first round, having earlier taken three long counts.

In his first nineteen contests, Downes won thirteen inside the distance and lost only three. His first defeat came at the hands of Dick Tiger, the tough Nigerian who later won the world middleweight title. It was Terry's third pro' battle, and he was caught by a savage left hook in the opening minute that laid him flat on his back. A more experienced man would have taken full advantage of the count, but not Downes. His dander was well up and he scrambled to his feet, eager for revenge, only to take another left that dropped him again.

When he got up at 'seven', a jagged cut over his left eye was streaming blood and there was a gash across his nose. Yet he gritted his teeth and tore into Tiger with increased fury. The fans then saw one of the fiercest fights for years, but, by the end of the sixth round, Terry's injured eye was in such bad shape that his seconds refused to allow him to continue.

It was a cut eye also that cost him his fight with Freddie Cross, and his third loss was to the now retired veteran Les Allen by a points decision which I shall always rank as among the most extraordinary I have seen. For I made Downes an easy winner.

When Terry forced Pat McAteer, the champion, to retire from the ring after taking an eight-round pounding in a non-title bout, it seemed obvious that 'Terrible Terry' was bound to be his successor.

So it proved at Harringay on 30 September 1958, when Downes battered the far more experienced Welsh champion, Phil Edwards, into submission in thirteen rounds to win the vacant crown. It was a masterpiece of calculated destruction, and he had become champion after only seventeen months campaigning as a professional and only twenty contests.

His opponents were usually so deluged midst a succession of jabs, hooks, uppercuts and crosses that they had time only for defence. Before long they would capitulate, physically and mentally demoralised. Downes loved fighting. He did not revel in easy victories; the tougher the opposition, the better. Even when he got licked, he still enjoyed every moment of the fracas.

Rather than sit in the dressing-room waiting to go on, he used to watch the preliminary bouts from a ringside seat. 'You only worry when you're waiting', Terry once told me. 'Watching the other fights gets me in the mood and my mind gets keyed up for the job of fighting. Beside, I learn a lot from watching others'. He preferred to meet those more experienced than himself. 'A little of the good always rubs off', he maintained.

This, then, was the crowd-pulling character for whom Jack Solomons was seeking an opponent for his first-ever promotion at Wembley on 9 December 1958, following the closing down of Harringay Arena. He wanted a high-ranking American, one from whom, if Downes emerged victorious, he would gain sufficient prestige to be ranked a genuine challenger for the world title.

The choice narrowed to three names, Ellsworth 'Spider' Webb, Joey Giardello and former world champion Gene Fullmer. Solomons finally decided on Webb, who had already made himself popular in this country by scoring a fine win over Dick Tiger at Earls Court. To make matters better still, from Solomons' point of view, Webb stopped Giardello in seven rounds, to earn promotion to third place in the world rankings.

Webb, a Negro, was born in Los Angeles on 20 November 1931. A brilliant performer as an amateur, he was a member of the 1952 American Olympic Games Team in which one of his fellow members was Floyd Patterson. 'The Spider' was beaten in the final of his event by Laszlo Papp of Hungary, only boxer to win three Olympic Gold Medals. He turned professional in the summer of 1953, since when he had lost only four bouts. He had vanquished such top-liners as Holly Mims, Rory Calhoun, Randy Sandy, Wilf Greaves and Jackie Labua and, in December 1956, had scored a one-sided victory over former British champion Pat McAteer in two rounds in Chicago.

It was common knowledge that Sugar Ray Robinson, the world champion, was none to anxious to put his title on the line against Webb who, besides being an extremely accomplished boxer, was not to be found lacking in the all-important matter of packing a wallop as well.

On the grounds of experience, Downes' chances did not appear too bright. Nor, if one took a line through the respective performances of the pair in their clashes with Tiger and McAteer, could 'The Paddington Whirlwind', as he was now dubbed, be favoured. On the morning of the fight, most of the experts forecast a win for Webb, basing their assumption on the grounds that he had well over five years' experience in the paid ring behind him, and that in top-class company, as against Terry's seventeen months and a mere twenty-two bouts.

As usual, promoter Solomons whetted the appetite of his customers with some excellent supporting contests and, before the main event came on at about nine-thirty, we saw Terry Spinks put up easily the outstanding performance of his career at that stage to cearly outpoint the formidable Canadian, Pat Supple. Then Empire featherweight champion Percy Lewis made sure that the fans remained in the right mood by making the highly-

ranked American, Carmelo Costa, appear nothing better than a 'hack'. Would Terry Downes be able to make it a double win for Britain over the two American stars?

That he did not do so was due more to the fact that,even then, we lived in a more humane age than the days when raw-fisted Britons fought on until they could not see, and then boxed on blind. I, for one, was glad when referee Eugene Henderson decided at the end of the eighth round that Downes--both eyes cut, nose leaking red life-blood--could not continue against the educated fists of Ellsworth 'Spider' Webb.

Downes tried to fight off the referee when he intervened because of his severely cut left eye, but I don't believe that there was another human in the vast audience who would have argued. The scene at the end of this fantastic fighting show went like this: Terry had patted Webb on the back and skipped back to his corner, where his seconds worked frantically to check cuts under both eyes and a gash above his nose.

The dusky Webb was slumped in his corner, grey-faced from exhaustion. When he saw Mr. Henderson visiting Downes' corner, he pushed aside his seconds and gazed anxiously to see what would happen.

When the referee signalled that the fight was over, Webb breathed in deeply and fell back into his corner. He was still staggering awkwardly, on unbelieving legs, when he rose to be named the winner. But who wants to see a willing horse spurred

to death? As I wrote this, in the immediate wake of this truly great fight and while my mind was still full of it, there was a nagging worry in my mind that Downes, the magnificent twenty-two-yearold, might have lost some of that vital spark of genius which made this one of the most memorable bouts ever staged in the famous Wembley ring. I only hoped that once again a truly bright British fistic star had not been called on to give too much too soon.

The battle, which was to provide so many sensations, started with one almost before the crowd had settled in their seats. Webb banged home a right-cross and Terry went down as though the very canvas had been whipped from under his feet.

He was on his knees at 'three', but there was bad hurt in his eyes. When he did rise at 'eight' his legs 'hose-piped' under him. For the rest of the round, Terry came in for savage punishment both to head and body and the cool and calm American almost toyed with him to the bell. It looked then as though Downes had been hopelessly overmatched. But at the end of the session he tapped Webb on the shoulder and, with a grin, informed him that he was heading for the wrong corner!

What happened after that remains a brave piece of British boxing history, recording a courage that was incredible. Downes flooded forward on magnificent waves of high-action. In the third a sickly grin smeared itself over Webb's puffed face, and I cannot ever remember seeing so many punches hurled so viciously.

As the men continued to beat savagely away at each other, the jungle note of the roaring crowd really began to introduce itself.

Webb was no longer the condescending professor teaching a pupil. It was he who was taking the caning, and he was very much on the retreat, eyes staring wildly from his alarmed face, as Downes bashed rights and lefts to the jaw that had the American shaking his head dispiritedly. Downes was up before the bell for the sixth round had ceased ringing. A left-right-left straight on the button of Webb's chin almost buckled the American wholly. Another blow then might have spelt curtains, but, as the Britisher pressed his luck, Webb showed his own amazing powers of recovery and caught Downes with hooks, uppercuts and swings to which Terry supplied counters on all parts of the target.

When they came out for the seventh I had Downes just ahead on my scorecard, but by the end of that round his left eye was bleeding badly and he was streaming blood from the nose. Now his best blows seemed to bounce off rather than to stagger Webb, but I thought that 'The Spider' had done no more than square the points by the time they left their corners for the eighth. And this, despite the fact that the referee had thought it necessary to examine Terry's eye during the interval before deciding to allow him to answer the next bell.

The eighth saw Webb, though obviously desperately tired, do almost all the forcing and Downes' face looked like an old, cracked and worn pillarbox, for now his other eye had gone, too. But he went to his corner prancing, proud and still very much erect. It was the referee who stopped him, not 'Spider' Webb, and it was the American who had to be almost carried up the aisle to his dressing room.

To make an epic fight the more complete, nothing either man said afterwards marred the earlier proceedings. Firstly, here are some Webb quotes: 'This was the toughest fight I have ever had, he really shook me. He is a very smart fighter, and should win a lot of prestige for British boxing. Terry would beat every boxer I have ever beaten, and I think one day he is certain to be world champion'. (Terry, of course, later turned Webb's prediction into ring history.)

Downes said: 'I lost and I'm not grumbling. I was taking it easy in the seventh and eighth in order to save something for the finish, and that's the last time I do anything silly like that. Anyway, I could do with a return and my manager needs the money!'

When I spoke to him the day after meeting Webb, super-fit Terry told me that he did not consider that this bruising battle would leave its mark on his future performances.

It didn't and, in July 1961, he beat America's Paul Pender to win the World Championship at the second attempt, even

though he lost the crown the following year, when the pair clashed for a third time.

And, late in 1964, he unsuccessfuly challenged for the lightheavyweight title in a pulsating match against Willie Pastrano of the U.S.A.

CHAPTER TWENTY: PETER KEENAN V. FREDDIE GILROY; FOR THE BRITISH AND EMPIRE BANTAMWEIGHT CHAMPIONSHIPS, IN KING'S HALL, BELFAST, ON 10 JANUARY, 1959.

'The King is dead, long live the King!' How apt this on the night of 10 January 1959, when, in the King's Hall, Belfast, local idol Freddie Gilroy deprived Glasgow's Peter Keenan of his British and Empire bantamweight titles. It was the end of the road for one who had been a great champion, yet the crowning of another whose frenzied followers fought to touch the hem of his garment.

A great champion. Yes, in my book Keenan was all of that. For in these modern times when big boxing is big business it is a rare occurrence to find a titleholder prepared to ply his wares anywhere on earth. Keenan's fistic epitaph should be: 'The World Was My Ring' for, in over ten years paid scrapping, he boxed in such widely separated places as Johannesburg, Belfast, Sydney (Australia), Marseilles, Manila and Paris. Not to mention all over Scotland, and in most of England's big halls.

Sure, with Peter boxing was a business, but he never picked 'em easy and seldom haggled over terms. He was self-managed during the latter part of his career, and he priced his services in accordance with the class of the suggested opposition and the importance of the proposed battle. Promoters needed only the briefest of negotiations with the little Scot. He

would state his terms, and it would be up to the impresario to say either 'yes' or 'no', or 'I'll think about it and let you know'.

Cut eyes were merely an occupational hazard to Peter and, during his career, he had some sixty stitches inserted in their vicinity as a result of wounds received in the ring. He won two Lonsdale Belts outright, besides annexing the European crown twice for brief spells and making five successful defences of the Empire title before dropping it to Gilroy. In all, he engaged in sixty-six contests as a professional, winning fifty-four, drawing one and losing eleven.

I first saw Keenan box in the final stages of the ABA Championships of 1948. He was then a flyweight, and he came to London as Scottish champion and a member of the Anderton Amateur Club. Peter was just short of his twentieth birthday then and, after winning his semi-final with comparative ease, he was on the wrong end of the verdict in the final against Henry Carpenter of the Bradfield Club, London. It was one of those bouts where the decision could quite fairly have gone either way--there are no 'draws' in amateur boxing--and luck did not favour the Scot.

I mention this to illustrate the point that amateurs of equal standing do not necessarily fare the same after they turn professional. There was nothing to choose between Keenan and Carpenter over the 'short sprint' distances as unpaids yet, as a

pro', Henry never reached great heights while Peter was at home from the very start.

And here is another strange thing. Though he was undoubtedly one of Britain's best champions of the post-war years, throughout Keenan's professional career he appeared in a London ring on no more than three occasions, none of them being in a title match. Bearing in mind the fact that in no less than seventeen of his bouts were titles at stake, that is indeed strange. It is only partly explained by the facts that he was a Scotsman and that, for many years, bantamweights had not been considered 'fashionable'.

Keenan was born on 8 August 1928, and he first punched for pay in September '48. By the end of 1950 he had established himself as official contender for Danny O'Sullivan's British eight stone six title, and remained undefeated after twenty-five contests. He created something of a sensation the following May by knocking out O'Sullivan in six rounds, and when he left for Johannesburg to challenge world champion Vic Toweel in January '52 he had extended his winning streak to thirty-two bouts, besides having taken the European championship from the Spaniard, Luis Romero. Though Peter failed against Toweel, he acquitted himself with credit, especially bearing in mind the strange surroundings plus the foreign climate and rarified air.

Perhaps that stint in the Union affected him more than he knew for, in his first bout after returning home, he was knocked

out in five rounds by Jean Sneyers of Belgium to drop the European title. And then, in October, Amleto Falcinelli forced him to retire in five rounds.

Followed a year of fluctuating fortunes for, in his first outing of 1953, Keenan successfully defended his British title for the second time--and in so doing won his first Lonsdale Belt outright--when he stopped northerner Frankie Williams in seven rounds at Paisley. After one more victory, he won back his European laurels when he outpointed Maurice Sandeyron in June, only to lose both these championships to the then up-and-coming John Kelly in Belfast four months later.

So Peter began 1954 tagged as no better than an 'ex-champion', but he did not allow such a state of affairs to continue for long. In February he whipped evergreen Eddie Carson over twelve rounds to win the Scottish title and, after a winning run in 'catchweight' bouts, Kelly was lured to Paisley for a return clash. This time, though, only the British title was at stake for John had, in the meantime, dropped the European crown to the French-Algerian, Robert Cohen.

This time it was obvious from the first bell that Kelly had no chance at all and Keenan, using his superior strength, bull-dozed his way to a knockout victory in the sixth round. Before the end of the year he had again visited Belfast, where he successfully defended his diadem against the Irish George O'Neill.

Keenan got off to a good start in the New year with a win over Dante Bini, a leading Continental, and then he made the long trek 'down-under' to outscore Australian champion Bobby Sinn for the vacant Empire title in March. Never one to rest on his laurels, Peter was not at his best in dropping a couple of points decisions to Continentals there before hitting the trail for home, but once back he did not hesitate to put the Empire crown on the line against the all-action little Zulu, Jake Tuli.

That meeting was an epic for, after looking all-in and a certain loser, the Scot pulled the fight out of the fire to win by a KO in the fourteenth round. The fight took place in Glasgow, and it was voted the finest encouter to take place in Scotland since Lynch beat Kane in 1937.

Peter had only three bouts in '56, but each one was far afield. Following a lay-off of ten months he returned to Sydney in October to stop the Aussies' new champion, Kevin James, in jig-time in an Empire title defence, and in November outpointed Frederico Scarponi of Italy in Melbourne. Then off the Manila, only to take the count in the ninth round of a battle with rugged Al Asuncion of the Philippines.

Four bouts, four wins, was Keenan's 1957 tally, and the year was particularly notable because one of these victories came in the sixth round of a British and Empire title match against fellow-Scot John Smillie. This success won Peter another Lonsdale Belt outright.

Looking back, it seems fair to record that 1958 saw Keenan's star on the wane. True, he lost only two of his six encounters, and true there were two winning Empire title defences against South Africa's Graham Van Der Walt and Canada'a Pat Supple. But critics were divided in their views on the merits of that verdict over Supple, and there could certainly have been little in it, for Peter did not find his true form until late in the bout. And though he looked good when defeating the veteran American, Billy Peacock, he was definitely unimpressive in losing to young Derry Treanor--even though it was a cut near the eye which caused him to be stopped in the sixth session. Finally, in November, Peter had to call on all his experience and craft in order to so much as stay the course in Paris against world champion Alphonse Halimi, in an overweight match. He was not credited as winning a single round in this one.

So it was that, on the day of the Keenan-Gilroy bout, forecasts varied as to the likely outcome. No one seemed to be able to make up their minds as to how much--if at all--Keenan had gone back. Chief reason for this was that he was known to be a far more formidable adversary when his titles were at stake, and some thought that his experience would see him through against the Belfast boy, who would be engaging in only his fourteenth paid contest.

Freddie was a two-fisted 'southpaw' and a crowd-pleaser even as an amateur. When hard-bitten pro' enthusiasts flock along to see a mere youngster in action, you can be sure he's got personality plus. Gilroy was first spotted at the age of nine, when he decided to become, in Belfast parlance, 'A Bosco Boy'. This meant that he joined the St. John Bosco Amateur Club, which was founded in the grim days of 1940 by a Roman Catholic Priest.

It was there that Gilroy met Jimmy McAree who was later to become his manager, and he took to the routine at the Bosco like a duck to water. By 1952, when Freddie went after his first title, McAree's tuition was paying off. In that year he won the six stone seven championship of Ulster, and then was ordered to temporarily hang up his gloves because McAree considered he was too light for the purposes of junior grade boxing.

'But there was no keeping him out', McAree once told me. 'And when I went along as a guest referee to a neighbouring club one evening and found that one of the boys I was expected to officiate over was Gilroy, what could I do other than give him my blessing?'

Season '53-54 was a great one for the fast-developing left-hander, for in quick succession he won the Ulster and Irish junior flyweight titles together with the Ulster senior flyweight championship. He would probably have cleared the board in 1955 but for the fact that injury kept him out of the Irish championships. For Christy Rafter, who annexed the title, met

Gilroy in his first outing as champ and was flattened inside a round.

The following year Freddie moved up a weight and boxed regularly for his country. As well as competing against all the other Home countries, he fought in Berlin (European Games), in Chicago (v. Golden Gloves champions), in Canada and in the Melbourne Olympics as well as going on tours of Germany. In additon to all these deeds, he captured the Irish championship.

Irish fight-fans were stunned when Freddie was not originally selected for the Melbourne trip, and so angry was the fighter at rumours that he was having weight trouble that he journeyed to Dublin at his own expense and undertook a public weigh-in. There and then a fund was launched to pay his passage to the Games, and when the Irish team set out Gilroy was with them.

At Melbourne, his knockout win over the star Russian Boris Stepanov, made the headlines the world over, but he was not destined to win a Gold Medal. Apart from his conqueror in the Games--Behrendt of Germany, who himself emerged as Gold Medalist--only three other men can claim victories over Gilroy in almost a century of amateur bouts.

Home again, Freddie did the obvious when he decided to discard his amateur singlet for good. But though offers to manage his affairs came from places as far afield as London and

Glasgow, Gilroy stuck to the man who had stuck to him and took McAree with him into the paid ranks in the role of 'pilot'.

In February '57 the 'Cloutin' Cherub', as baby-faced Freddie had come to be affectionately known by this time, burst into the pro' game with a startling win in two minutes flat over Derek McReynolds, who must have thought that the Ulster Hall had been struck by lightning. And by the time he stepped in with Keenan, the Irishman was undefeated after thirteen bouts, only four of his opponents having stayed long enough to give the referee the formality of totting up his scorecard.

Outstanding among Gilroy's perfomances were a comfortable points margin over West Hartlepool's George Bowes in an eliminator fought on the northerner's 'own midden', an eight-round success on Johnny Morrissey's retiring in the final eliminator at Glasgow, a four-round KO of Pierre Cossemyns of Belgium (one-time conqueror of Hogan (Kid) Bassey), and a seventh round triumph against George O'Neill who, as mentioned earlier, had stayed the full fifteen rounds with Keenan in a title match.

The only real doubt concerning the Belfast boy arose through his hands, both of which were brittle and had caused him trouble on a number of occasions. Because Freddie carried a dose of anaesthetic in either glove, there was always the chance that he might damage his own fists if any of his blows found a hard target.

Seldom can a champion have shown more courage in defeat than did Keenan before some 16,000 happy Irishmen, and never can a loser have displayed a finer spirit of sportsmanship. It was fitting that, when he announced his retirement from the ring immediately following his reverse, those who had rapturously greeted Gilroy's victory with 'When Irish Eyes are Smiling' stood in tribute to a great fighter and sang the wistful words of 'Auld Lang Syne'. I was never more moved at a ringside.

The proceedings were halted just one second before the end of the eleventh round with the two-pound heavier Scot utterly and hopelessly beaten. The wonder was that he had held out for so long, for from the outset of the contest it had been clear that he had neither the speed nor the punch to cope with a youngster who hit with the speed of a striking cobra and with the power of a steam-hammer.

Keenan withstood a severe battering in round after round and was on the floor several times, but he used every trick in the book to stave off defeat. Every legitimate artifice--and a few that the rule-book frowns on--were employed by the champion. He rarely obeyed the refeee's command to 'break', waiting instead for Gilroy to push him off.

All his efforts may have gained him a little breathing-space, but otherwise they availed him little. Freddie's right-hand jabs had the Scot's left eye looking sore from the opening round and, in the third, after landing a volley of hooks to the head, he had blood seeping from the champion's right eye.

It was in this round that Keenan first hit the floor, and it was a powerful left and right to the chin that put him there. He rose at once, but another vicious assault had him so shaken that when the bell went he was clutching Gilroy grimly round the waist. It was only rarely that the Belfast boxer had to take a blow to the head, but Keenan nailed him with some lovely right counters to the stomach--and took a lot of violent abuse in reply!

Invariably, when he sank his right into Freddie's midriff, he was assaulted with half-a-dozen savage hooks and uppercuts before he could withdraw, and several times he was sent reeling into the ropes, on one occasion almost plunging through them.

In the eighth Gilroy suddenly erupted into violent activity, and after an all-out attack he sank a murderous left hook into the older man's ribs. Peter involuntarily drew up his knees as pain seared his body and down he went amid a tumult of sound, rising like a man mounting a gallows at 'eight'. He was promptly driven across the ring and fell again in the Irishman's corner, but rose at 'two' and somehow managed to weather the storm till the bell.

The ninth and tenth saw the Scot hit with a multitude of punches, but he was cool enough and skilful enough to duck or ride the most deadly of the lethal blows that buzzed about his

head. Bruised, battered but rarely bewildered, the Scottish champion gave everything he had--but it just wasn't enough.

Gilroy opened the eleventh by driving Keenan into a neutral corner and felling him for 'three'.Then another vicious battery of blows to the Scot's head and body sent him crashing on his back. Up at 'nine' but very groggy, the champion was the victim of yet another terrific assault and took four of five full-blooded thumps on the chin before going down again.

Courageously, he made to rise at 'seven', almost falling back as he levered himself up only to be smacked on the side of the face by a left which put him on hands and knees as the bell rang. It transpired that, amid the earsplitting din, referee Bill Williams had ordered Gilroy to: 'Stop boxing, that's enough' as Keenen was about to fall. Therefore the bout was over. A champion had gone down to glorious defeat and a new young king reigned in his place.

It was a candid Keenan who spoke to me shortly afterwards in his dressing-room. 'He should be a fine champion', he said of Gilroy. 'He's fast and clever, and if anybody doubts that he punches as hard as he's supposed to, they should have been where I was tonight!'

Nursing, as usual, hands that were sore after the terrific battering they had handed out, Freddie Gilroy was the least excited of all those gathered around him. 'I hope to be as good a

champion as Keenan was', he said gravely, adding with a grin: 'and I hope to make as much money as he did!'

From first to last Peter Keenan was a credit both to himself and to the sport he represented. He went out like a champion.

CHAPTER TWENTY-ONE: BRIAN LONDON V. HENRY COOPER; FOR THE HEAVYWEIGHT CHAMPIONSHIPS OF GREAT BRITAIN AND THE BRITISH EMPIRE, AT THE EXHIBITION HALL, EARLS COURT, ON 12 JANUARY, 1959.

If you have twin sons, birthday presents provide knotty problems. The father of Bellingham's Henry and George Cooper got over the difficulty, when his offspring reached the age of five, by giving each a pair of boxing gloves. Now they could spar together.

The first session proved disastrous, for George hit his elder brother (Henry was born just twenty minutes earlier on 23 May 1934) on the nose and knocked him down. The back of his head struck the kitchen floor and Henry took the count. The gloves were promptly confiscated, but the seed had been sown and the Cooper twins grew to love boxing. And when, at the age of twelve, they were allowed to join a Youth Club which specialised in fistic tuition, their happiness was complete.

Yet is was not until they were called up for National Service that they really blossomed out into promising amateurs. By coincidence, they came into the RAOC unit in which I was running the boxing team. George competed among the heavyweights, while Henry played havoc among the lightheavies. Though these identical twins could scarcely be told apart outside the ring, Henry's class now stood out a mile inside it.

Twice he was Army and Inter-Services champion and, in 1952 and '53, he won the ABA lightheavyweight crown. He represented England in the 1952 Olympic Games at Helsinki, only to get licked by a Russian in the second series.

I well remember that, at about this time, Henry's increasing weight was causing embarrassment. For he was determined to get down to the lightheavy limit at championship time, purely to give his brother the opportunity of gaining honours in the heavyweight class!

Henry Cooper, blue-eyed and handsome, stood six-foot-one-and-a-half in his stockinged feet and, at just over thirteen-and-a-half-stone, he had an ideal build for a heavyweight. But this quiet and unassuming Londoner, who had the courage, determination and ambition to overcome even the most disappointing of setbacks and who first punched for pay in October '54, got to the top the hard way. Though his debut minus amateur singlet made fighting for cash appear simple, for he gained a one-round win over experienced Harry Painter to set the Harringay fans roaring.

Henry continued in fine style until the spring of '55, when he met his first reverse at the hands of Italy's Uber Bacilleri, who cut his eye so badly that the bout had to be ended in the second round. Up to this time, only two opponents had succeeded in so much as staying the distance with the 'Bellingham Basher', one

of them being Joe Bygraves of Jamaica, who was nonetheless clearly outscored at Manor Place Baths, Walworth.

By the end of the year Henry had reversed the decision against Bacilleri, but had gone under on a close points verdict to his old amateur rival, Joe Erskine, in an 'eliminator'. If the following year was not exactly a busy one, at least it was sensational. After stopping Maurice Mols of France in four rounds, promoter Freddie Mills paired Cooper in a 'natural' against the then-unbeaten Brian London. This was a real revenge battle, for a few months earlier his brother--who used 'Jim' as a ringname--had been walloped by the 'Blackpool Blockbuster'.

Sitting ringside with yours truly, Henry had watched his twin fight desperately against London's all-out attack, and afterwards he promised 'Jim' that he would make Brian pay dearly for his win. And how he kept his word, for, before London knew what it was all about, Henry had tagged him with a dazzling left hook that scattered his fighting wits and caused the referee to rescue Brian in the opening round.

But in September he suffered another eye injury that cost him a fight he was winning against northerner Peter Bates. So worried did Henry become about his apparent susceptibility to cuts that he became over-cautious in the ring--a failing which, I believe, led to his downfall in bouts which he might otherwise have won.

Former victim Joe Bygraves, Empire champion now but under-dog in the betting for his defence against Cooper in February '57, slammed in a mighty blow to the body which dropped his challenger for the full count in the ninth round but, three months later, Henry got a wonderful chance to regain prestige by meeting the European champion, Ingemar Johansson, in Sweden. Ultra-caution again sent him into his shell and he was knocked out in the fifth round.

He was still hesitant when he stepped in again with Erskine, this time with the British title, which Joe had annexed from Johnny Williams, at stake. That was in September '57, and again Cooper finished second.

Lack of work here sent Cooper to Germany for three bouts, and there he regained something like his real form. Hanz Kalbfell was easily outpointed, huge Heinz Neuhaus was on the lucky end of a drawn decision. Then, after dropping Erich Schoeppner for the full count in the sixth round, the referee had second thoughts and caused the M.C. to announce that Cooper had been disqualified because his final punch had landed on the German's neck!

Now Henry was back in the picture, and it came as no surprise when, at the end of the summer of '58, he was paired with Dick Richardson in a Porthcawl clash to determine a challenger for new champion Brian London, who had recently dethroned Erskine. But when Cooper's old eye-wound re-opened, his nose poured blood, and he was battered down for a long count in a neutral corner, it looked like the end.

I contend that Cooper was one of those rare fighters who are most dangerous when their backs are to the wall. He rose to catch the burly Welshman with a smashing right under the heart, and, with that one blow, Henry turned 'killer' instead of being the victim. Dynamite-laden left hooks and accurate right crosses dropped Dick for 'eight' in the fifth and, soon after he rose, referee Ike Powell stepped between the pair to name Cooper the winner.

Despite that glorious triumph, not a single critic gave Henry even an outside chance when he tackled Zora Folley at Wembley in October. Folley was at the time rated by the Americans as number one contender to world champion Floyd Patterson, but Henry again overcame the disadvantages of a knockdown and a cut eye to score a brilliant points victory through left hand boxing.

As Brian London had, a fortnight previously, also defeated a leading American in the person of Willie Pastrano, there was tremendous public demand for a London-Cooper return with the former's titles at stake. And as London was dead-keen to prove that his earlier reverse at Cooper's hands was just a mistake, Jack Solomons was able to clinch the match for January 1959 at the Exhibition Hall, Earls Court, which had a

seating capacity of 18,001, and so was Britain's largest indoor fight arena.

The pairing was made unique by the fact that it represented the first-ever meeting of British heavyweights both of whom were currently rated in America as being among the world's top ten big men.

Officially Brian had no manager, but it was common knowledge that his father, Jack senior--himself a former British and Empire title-holder--had a big say in his son's business affairs.

Brian was born to the fighting family Harper, of West Hartlepools, on 19 June 1934, elder brother Jack junior having arrived a year beforehand. Dad had already adopted the ringname 'London' and had so far engaged in fifty-nine contests to assist in earning the rent and keeping the wolf from the door. Remember, those were the bad old days of unemployment.

At the age of ten, Brian had what he still ranks as his biggest boxing thrill. This came, when, with their mother, the brothers went to Belle Vue, Manchester, and watched Pop win the titles in a scrap with Freddie Mills. Less than a year later there were tears as they watched him lose his laurels through being knocked out in the sixth round by Bruce Woodcock on the 'Spurs Football Ground.

Brian did not box at all until he entered the Royal Air Force to undergo his period of National Service, and he has

disclosed that he only volunteered for the unit boxing team then because he 'thought it would mean no fatigues'.

Of his first fifteen bouts, all but one were won by knockouts, but in them London or Harper, as he was known then, appeared as some strange kind of runaway windmill. Even so, he was selected to represent his Service, and within three years of engaging in his first serious bout had collected the RAF, Imperial Services, Britannia Shield, ABA and Empire Games titles. In all his amateur bouts Brian dropped only three decisions--one of them being to Joe Erskine.

The Vancouver Empire Games made a fitting climax to London's unpaid ring days, and it was a wonderful moment for him when he was presented with a winner's Gold Medal by the Duke of Edinburgh. Then, suddenly, his RAF days were over and he had to choose between going back to his steady but well-paid job of lettering the famous seaside rock in Blackpool, or taking the risks and financial rewards of the prize ring.

'The thought of the money and the security the ring might one day bring finally decided me, but I gave it a deal of thought first', Brian told me once.

So, as Brian London, he made his debut among the professionals at the Royal Albert Hall on 23 March 1955. The proceedings on this occasion were brief in the extreme, for Denis Lockton lasted only two minutes fifty-six seconds, of which he spent twenty-six seconds on the canvas before the referee

decided that he had taken enough. A critic who had never before seen the Blackpool lad in action labelled him: 'A crude swinger with no knowledge of the noble art, yet blessed with a pay-off punch'.

After Brian had gone through twelve bouts undefeated (only a Belgian named Robert Eugene was still there at the final bell) the experts changed their tune. Now he was freely described as being the heavyweight prospect of the century, so the announcement of the first fight with Cooper came as no surprise. Now hear Brian's side of the story.

'Brother Jack was on the bill as well as me, and he went on early in the programme. I was left alone in the dressing-room while everyone went to watch him. I worked myself into such a state that I don't recall going into the ring, let alone leaving it........stangely enough next day, instead of being depressed, my one ambition was to get back into a ring, and I have never since suffered from pre-fight nerves'.

Three wins scored in a total of less than eight rounds followed the Cooper reverse, and then even a disputed points loss to Heinz Neuhaus in Germany failed to halt the London progress. After a further three quick KO's, Brian took the fight-scribes by surprise when, by way of a change, he handed out a boxing lesson to the Tongan, Kitione Lave, to win the decision by a street. Four months later he did likewise to Howie Turner of America.

On 25 February 1958, Brian topped the Harringay card in his first memorable clash with Willie Pastrano, and referee Bill Williams' decision in favour of the American was hotly disputed. Though I agreed with the referee--for once!--it was certainly close and we had our breath taken away at the speed and power of London's display. His bulldozing tactics completely upset the usually so composed Willie.

Next on the London agenda was a title bout with Joe Erskine. 'Dad told met not to worry if Erskine went ahead on points', Brian has disclosed. 'He told me to keep moving forward and that well within the scheduled fifteen rounds I would nail him and knock him out. Well, I nailed him good in the seventh and finished him off in the eighth'.

A return with Pastrano was inevitable, especially as the Londons had nothing but confidence as to what the outcome of such a fight would be. Yet, again, the newspapermen made the American a red-hot favourite for the bout which was fought at Harringay on the last day of September.

'I suspected that Pastrano would concentrate his attack on my body, and so we worked on a cross-counter during training. In the third round I caught him squarely with just about the hardest right I ever threw, and I was amazed that he didn't go down. After that I felt him weakening and I was sorry that his cut eye ended it after the fifth. There's no way of proving it, but I felt I would have stopped him anyway about the eighth--and that would have been much more satisfactory'. The above are quotes from my notes, jotted down, word for word, in Brian's dressing-room immediately after the fight.

That, then, was the state of the poll as we fight-lovers eagerly awaited the second collison of London and Cooper.

Henry trained in his usual quarters--the gymnasium of the Thomas A'Beckett Inn, down the Old Kent Road, while Brian got into shape at his old RAF camp, Weeton. The Press gave the fight a tremendous build-up, and it was certainly the most controversial battle involving the British heavyweight title since Jack Petersen and Jack Doyle met in 1933. I am writing now, of course, of the situation before the fight, for while Petersen v. Doyle ended in fiasco, London v. Cooper was certainly one of the finest, if one-sided, clashes between big men ever to be fought in a British ring.

On the day of the fight most of the experts went out on a limb in their predicitions that London would win. *Daily Express* columnist, Desmond Hackett, wrote a particularly powerful piece, which was illustrated with a full-face photograph of Cooper, the scars above and below his left eyebrow being specially indicated. Des was only one of the daily paper scribes who forecast a win for London round about the half-way stage in the scheduled fifteen-rounder.

At the weigh-in, I bumped into Joe Erskine who, at the same time as the Cooper twins, had served in the unit where I was myself stationed in the RAOC. Joe, as I have mentioend earlier, had met both Henry and Brian as professionals. In addition, he had clashed with Cooper three times and London once in the amateur ranks.

Erskine was among the few who forecast a win for Cooper......'he is the harder puncher and the better boxer.....and he is used to conceding weight'. (Henry came in at 13 stone ten-and-a-half to London's 14 stone thirteen-and-one-quarter).

And that night the new champion, Henry Cooper, stood blood-soaked and battered as Ike Powell named him the winner after a fight that was breathtaking in its savagery. The Bellingham boxer won with a steel-tough left that matched in durability his fighting heart, for had he not looked like a crudely-slaughtered beast by the seventh round? Then he had been a crimsoned, shattered-looking athlete with blood cascading from his nose, left eye cut and swollen and looking like a turtle's egg.

As early as the second round Cooper was bleeding from the nose and there was a graze by London's left eye. In the sixth, Henry began to bleed from the left eyebrow and in the seventh he was cut under the same eye.

In the ninth, London's left eye started to swell to trombone-size proportions, and in the tenth his right eye, which had previously been swelling, burst like a punctured blood-orange. Then, in the eleventh, Cooper's other eye went.

I list all these injuries only to show how desperately each man tried, and how both refused to bow the knee to the physical distress which can come upon two men, armed only with leather gloves.

Though the exchanges turned out to be one-sided, it was only in the second half of the fight that it became obvious who was going to win. True, London lost the first four rounds on the trot. Yet so phenomenal was his strength that, although one lost count of the number of left jabs, leads and hooks that thudded home, it seemed impossible for Cooper to halt the champion's lumbering, but infinitely menacing advance.

In the fifth, I thought I discerned signs that the tide was turning. London, for once, beat his man to the punch and a left and a right hurt Cooper, who was pinned in a corner. He missed wildly when he tried to fight his way out, and a right landed on the side of his head and sent him down for 'two'. This was the only time either man went to the boards during the whole of the forty-five minutes boxing.

For the next three rounds the battle was in the balance. Cooper continued to throw his lefts as he had done from the start, but now they seemed to have as much chance of halting London as has a pea-shooter of stopping a tank.

Cooper was way out in front at the half-way mark, but the cut under his eye looked like a raw kidney, livid and swelling. Then, in the ninth, it suddenly became clear that not only was the

champion dropping further and further behind on points, but that the strength was slowly draining out of him.

From that point on Brian was the pupil of the ruthless master of the left hand. By the twelfth, the cut by London's right eye was bleeding worse than any of the many which criss-crossed Cooper's face like the tracks of a railway junction. Yet the big man kept coming forward, though such a policy was now obviously to his inevitable doom.

I almost wished that Henry could, from somewhere or another, produce a really refrigerating punch in the thirteenth, for the fading champion was like a bullock who has a date with a slaughterman armed with a blunt axe. His face seemed to be a magnet for Cooper's left, and only his heart remained unaffected by the punishment he was absorbing.

So bemused was the Blackpool man that, at the end of the fourteenth, he raised Cooper's arm in token of victory, clearly thinking that the fight was over. One can imagine his feelings when he found that there was another round still to so!

As the title edged away from his son with almost every punch thrown, Brian's father sank his face into his hands and brother Jack screamed advice. London may have heard, but he was powerless to act, for there was always that tormenting left prying into his face, jabbing endlessly and then hooking murderously into the crimson wreck that was London's right eye.

Yet Brian struggled on until, at last, the final bell brought his frustrating torture to an end. The referee's decision was, of course, a mere formality, but it was a trifle delayed because Mr. Powell was unable to attract Cooper's attention for a few seconds. Henry, you see, was too busy commiserating with and receiving congratulatons from the man he had vanquished.

As anyone interested in British boxing knows, Cooper's career went from strength to strength, with only half-a-dozen setbacks along the way, until his eventual final retirement in 1971. He won three Lonsdale Belts outright through engaging in no less than ten winning battles for the British title, and he held the European crown on three separate occasions between 1964 and 1971.

And, of course, he boxed Cassius Clay twice (both times before 'The Greatest's' exile from the ring and return as Muhammad Ali). The first time, when Clay/Ali was still uncrowned as World Champion through being avoided like the plague by Sonny Liston, was a scheduled ten-rounder at Wembley Stadium and this was the occason when Henry so nearly won by a knockout at the end of the fourth round, only to be stopped through a cut eye in the fifth.

The second meeting involved the World Championship which Clay/Ali had taken off Liston in 1964 and already defended three times. It went on at Highbury, the home of Arsenal Football Club, in May 1966 and, although Cooper gave an excellent

account of himself, he was finally halted, yet again with cuts, in the sixth round.

Our 'Enry's ring days finally came to an end when he was controversially outpointed by Joe Bugner in March 1971, and thus deprived of all his titles, British, Empire and European, after fifteen enthralling rounds.

Though Brian London's subsequent career was less distinguished, against the orders of the B.B.B. of C. he was given a shot at the then holder of the World Championship, Floyd Patterson, in May 1959 in Indianopolis, USA, being knocked out in the eleventh round after boxing purely defensively throughout.

Lucky old London! Three months after Cooper's world title challenge, promoter Solomons enticed Clay over here one more time to give London his chance at Earls Court. The bout was something of a debacle for, after failing to land a worthwhile punch on his elusive foe, Brian was knocked out somewhat ignominiously in the third round.

Yet still he fought on, finally retiring from the ring only after being stopped by Bugner, when Joe was still on his way up, in May 1970.